The Identity of Literature

The Identity of Literature

A Reply to Jacques Derrida

Rajnath

RAWAT PUBLICATIONS
Jaipur • New Delhi • Bangalore • Guwahati • Kolkata

ISBN 978-81-316-0899-9

Published by
Prem Rawat for **Rawat Publications**
Satyam Apts, Sector 3, Jawahar Nagar, Jaipur 302 004 (India)
Phone: 0141 265 1748 / 7006 Fax: 0141 265 1748
E-mail: info@rawatbooks.com
Website: www.rawatbooks.com

New Delhi Office
4858/24, Ansari Road, Daryaganj, New Delhi 110 002
Phone: 011 2326 3290

Also at *Bangalore, Guwahati* and *Kolkata*

Typeset by Rawat Computers, Jaipur
Printed at Nice Printing Press, New Delhi

For my granddaughter
Khushi
and my grandson
Vishesh
for all those moments of joy
that they have given me.

Contents

Preface

This is not a book on Jacques Derrida or his deconstruction: it is a critique of Derrida on literature. Derrida denies that literature has any distinct identity and merges it with philosophy, history and other disciplines. To him, all texts are without any specificity and all are literary in nature. This has made philosophers uncomfortable but literary critics have by and large enjoyed this expansion of literature and proliferation of literariness.

Derrida's deconstruction has resulted in the death of literature in the conventional sense which gave it a pride of place in the domain of humanities, social sciences as well as pure sciences. Philosophers have been trying to separate their discipline from literature but no serious effort has been made by literary critics to separate literature from philosophy. Even Alvin Kernan in his *The Death of Literature* makes no effort to salvage the identity of literature from deconstruction but merely demonstrates the situation of literature in the postmodern era.

Philosophers have been more serious than literary critics in saving the identity of their discipline. Jürgen Habermas, the German philosopher, makes a sincere and serious attempt in his 'Levelling the Genre Distinction between Philosophy and Literature' and other writings to separate the two disciplines in order to establish a distinct identity of philosophy. The present work is a similar effort from the side of literature. I sincerely hope that the book will be appreciated for what it has rather than be criticized for what it has not, as it excludes a number of things which are not of any concern.

In the writing of the book I have been helped by Prof. Arthur Efron (Buffalo, USA), Prof. K. Narayan Chandran (Hyderabad) and Prof. L.R. Sharma (Allahabad) for which they deserve special mention and thanks.

This book could not have been written without the unstinting cooperation from my wife, Lata.

Rajnath

Chapter 1

Philosophy, Literature and Literary Criticism

The identity of literature has been under erosion ever since the demise of the New Criticism. The two-language theory first upheld by the Russian formalists and later reinforced by the New Critics, was replaced by the one-language theory.

The transition took place in the mid-1960s when Derrida emerged on the scene alongwith the reader-response critics. Both questioned the two-language theory, the former asserting that there is only one language which is literary and the latter arguing that there is only one language which becomes ordinary or literary depending on the reading conventions used. But there is a difference between them. The reader-response critics admit the existence of literature as distinct from non-literature, even though this is generated by the reader who can transform any piece of ordinary writing into literature. Derrida, on the other hand, flatly denies that there is any ordinary language or writing as whatever is written is literature.

Deconstruction emerged on the American critical scene around 1970 when Paul de Man published his critical essays and his widely acclaimed book of deconstructive criticism, *Blindness and Insight* (1971). In the mid-1970s started translations of Derrida's works into English. The first to come out was *Of Grammatology* (1967) translated by Gayatri Chakravorty Spivak in 1974 followed by *Writing and Difference* (1967) translated by Alan Bass in 1978. These were two major works by Derrida, which established his reputation in the English-speaking world. In the early 1980s, books on deconstruction started coming out beginning with Christopher Norris's *Deconstruction: Theory and Practice* (1982) and Jonathan Culler's *On Deconstruction* (1983). By the mid-1980s deconstruction was all the rage.

It is interesting to note that Derrida, a philosopher by training, was taken more seriously by literary critics than by philosophers who felt that by denying logic and truth, which used to be the prime concerns of philosophy, he had dealt a death blow to their discipline. Literary critics, on the other hand, embraced deconstruction under the impression that it was a proliferation of literariness. Even a perceptive critic like Murray Krieger lauds deconstruction saying that 'instead of the concept of literature being deconstructed into *ëcriture, ëcriture* has been constructed into literature.' (Seturaman, 539). What Krieger fails to realize is that by merging literature with *ëcriture* and vice versa deconstruction had taken away its independent identity.

Yale University was the hub of the New Criticism that gave birth to a new approach to literature with an exclusive focus on the text by which was meant literary text. A sharp distinction was made by the New Critics between literature and other disciplines or, for that mater, literary and ordinary language and the identity of literature was clearly defined. Although the New Critics were not familiar with the Russian formalists, they were the first to adopt the formalistic approach to literature. Writing in the second and third decades of the twentieth century, they not only focused on the text and distinguished between the familiar language of non-literature and the defamaliarized language of literature, in the fashion of the New Critics, they also viewed the function of criticism as identification of literariness. Roman Jakobson, the pivotal figure in Russian formalism, said:

> The object of the science of literature is not literature, but literariness—that is, that which makes a given work a work of literature. (Qtd. in Eichenbaum, 107)

As if anticipating Derrida, the Russian formalists maintained that the main source of literariness is not imagery (read metaphor) but rhythm in poetry and plot structure in fiction.

Why did the Yale critics who were brilliant students of literature accept deconstruction without questioning? Was it their irresistible attraction towards something altogether unconventional in the domain of philosophy, which they could assimilate and apply to literary texts? Was it their intense desire to distance themselves from the New Critics who were rather conventional in their view of literature and literary language? The New Critics were designated neo-Coleridgeans, as many of their critical postulates were derived from Coleridge. I.A. Richards, who exercised a decisive impact on them, had done a book-length study of Coleridge's theory of imagination.[1] At the other end of the spectrum, Paul de Man had done a deconstructive reading of

Coleridge and the New Critics in his *Blindness and Insight*, little realizing the differences between them and the deconstructionists.[2] It was de Man rather than Derrida who was followed by the American deconstructionists.

In course of time, deconstruction took the world by storm and Derrida emerged as an intellectual giant with more and more disciplines and individuals coming under his influence. Surprisingly enough, the focus shifted from literature to philosophy so much so that what Derrida said about literature was at times not even taken cognizance of. One reason for this may be that the real confrontation of the deconstructionists was with the conservative philosophers rather than the literary critics. And humanistic critics like Cleanth Brooks, Murray Krieger, M.H. Abrams, etc. who initially took issue with the deconstructionists did not put up a fight on solid ground. They slowly receded into the background with some of them passing away.

The critical movement that emerged with or after deconstruction such as reader-response criticism, postcolonial theory and new historicism were in consonance with the deconstructive position that there was no difference between literature and non-literature. The reader-response critics propounded their theory of one language with two manifestations, which was essentially not different from Derrida's one-language theory. Although they accepted the identity of literature, for them this could be discerned in any ordinary discourse. Postcolonial theory, which was a major movement after deconstruction, bypassed the questions relating to language, literariness and the identity of literature, except occasional remarks in their writings. Edward Said, Gayatri Chakravorty Spivak and Homi Bhabha were primarily concerned to foreground the manifested or latent colonial content of texts. New historicism viewed all texts, literary and non-literary, as forming the cultural climate of an age as its products as well as producers. For them, literary, historical, political and other texts alike contributed to the *zeitgeist* of the period and were alike in nature.

Why is it necessary to oppose deconstruction when it has become so pervasive? For me, there are two strong reasons for setting myself in opposition to Derrida and the other deconstructionists; first, to establish the independent identity of literature and secondly, to establish the logic in literature as well as other forms of writing. The two are correlated. Derrida dissolves the distinction between literature and other disciplines in order to establish that language as such is literature. From this Derrida concludes that there is no language which can communicate logic and truth which are not the concerns of literature. By marking literature off from other disciplines and literary language from ordinary language, the present work argues that there is a language of literature which is distinct from the language of non-literature and that even the language of literature is not altogether deprived of logic.

The real opposition to Derrida came from philosophers, not literary critics who were either ill-quipped to answer him or wellowed in the ubiquity of literariness that his deconstruction spawned. But philosophers were ruthless in their attack on Derrida for rejecting logic and truth which were always at the centre of their discipline. One may refer to German philosopher Hans-Georg Gadamer's magisterial *Truth and Method* (1980), which examines the norms by which one may grasp the meaning of a text. Derrida had a debate with Gadamer at the Goethe Institute in Paris in April 1981. Gadamer made his point forcefully and asserted that the ability to

> understand is the fundamental endowment of man, one that sustains his communal life with others and above all one that takes place by way of language and the partnership of conversation. (Qtd. in Mikics, 185)

This is against the spirit of Derrida who thinks that between two individuals only misunderstanding is possible. The language which is at the disposal of man is incapable of communicating any objective logic without which truth cannot be arrived at. Gadamer's arguments were incontrovertible and Derrida's response was very brief either deliberately, out of disdain, as Gadamer felt (Mikics, 187) or he found it difficult to answer him.

French philosopher Paul Ricoeur's stupendous *The Rule of Metaphor* published in 1975 (translated into English in 1977) is a solid demolition of Derrida views in 'White Mythology' published in 1971 (translated into English in 1974). Setting metaphor and metaphysics against each other, Derrida denies logic in metaphor which pervades philosophical as well as literary texts. As against Derrida, Ricoeur argues that metaphor is not without logic. Derrida denies reference which is synonymous with logic, truth, God, etc. in all discourses, including literature and philosophy. Suppression of reference which is a characteristics of metaphor results in deconstructive aporia which flies in the face of truth. Ricoeur admits the referential suppression in metaphor but goes beyond Derrida to argue that out of the death of reference, another reference is born. He asks a rhetorical question:

> Can one say that, by drawing *a new semantic pertinence out of the ruins of the literal meaning,* the metaphoric interpretation *also* sustains a new referential design, through those same means of abolition of the reference corresponding to the literal interpretation of the statement? (230, the first emphasis added)

This is a phoenix-like death and rebirth of reference in metaphor. For example, 'man is wolf' sounds illogical, if taken literally because there is no similarity between the two in shape or sound, but it does make sense at the level of the secondary reference which compares the qualities of man and wolf: man is cunning like a wolf.

Ricoeur refutes Derrida's deconstruction by positing a radical distinction between dead metaphors and living metaphors. Derrida's deconstruction is the outcome of the 'metaphorical sedimentation' or 'metaphorical credentials' of language. For Derrida, fading of the metaphorcity of language resulted in metaphysics and its resuscitation will uproot metaphysics with all its logic and reason. A clear distinction between living and dead metaphors is made by Ricoeur in order to establish 'the discontinuity between speculative and poetic discourse.' (258) Ricoeur asserts that 'dead metaphors are no longer metaphors but instead are associated with literal meaning.' (290)

Ricoeur's fine distinction between philosophy and literature or what he calls 'discontinuity between speculative and poetic discourse' was not paid much attention by the academics in the English-speaking world, especially the USA, as they were so enamoured of Derrida and so impressed by the novelty of his thought that they were not inclined to accept anything against him. But another philosopher, this time a German, put up a tough fight with Derrida and succeeded in dethroning him from his royal position as an intellectual. Jürgen Habermas, around the same age as Derrida, pleaded for logic and reason without which no communication is possible. The very fact that communication takes place between individuals and individuals and society disproves Derrida's deconstruction.

In his chapter on 'Leveling the Genre Distinction between Philosophy and Literature' in *The Philosophical Discourse of Modernity* (1985, translated into English, 1987), Habermas interrogates Derrida on his main thesis which is contained in the following pronouncement:

> No internal criticism can guarantee the essential 'literariness' of a text. There is no assured essence or existence of literature. If you proceed to analyse all the elements of a literary work you will never come across literature itself only some traits which it shares or borrows which you can find elsewhere too, in other texts, be it a matter of the language, the meaning, or the referents. (73)

Habermas's main objection is that Derrida reduces all manifestations of language to a single language which is literary. He finds three different forms of language: first, the language of day-to-day communication; secondly, the language of science, morality and law as well as social sciences; and thirdly, the language of literature. He distinguishes between the problem-solving capacities of language in science and social science and its world disclosive capacity in literature, especially poetry. Commenting upon the two opposite directions in which the ordinary language of daily communication moves, Habermas writes:

> In modern societies the spheres of science, morality and law have crystallized around these forms of argumentation. The corresponding cultural systems of action administer *problem solving capacities* in a way similar to that in which the enterprises of art and literature administer *capacities for world disclosure*. Because Derrida *overgeneralizes* this one linguistic function, namely the poetic, he can no longer see the complex relationship of the ordinary practice of normal speech to the two extraordinary spheres differentiated, as it were, in opposite directions. (30, the third emphasis added)

This is a very sane and sensible view of language which suitably answers Derrida's unduly simplistic view which sees language only in one form. Habermas is right when he says that Derrida 'overgeneralizes' the literary or poetic function of language. The multiplicity of forms that language takes has been overlooked by Derrida who only sees that language is the common medium of literature as well as non-literature and that language is literary.

It is unfortunate that literary critics who are better equipped than philosophers to appreciate literature and literariness have not grappled with Derrida and the Derrideans at close quarters to salvage the identity of literature. Philosophers have always been deficient in their response to literature barring a couple of them. Plato was the first philosopher who wrote about literature. There is no doubt that he asked some important and relevant questions about the nature and function of literature, but his answers were mostly wrong. In *The Republic*, which is a classic of philosophy, he dwells at length on literature and employs an analogy which is often used in literary discussions. Literature, he says, is a mirror of reality which is already an imitation of the reality created by God and, thus, it 'stands at third remove from reality.' (1974: 425) In this significant pronouncement, the first part is acceptable while the second part is highly questionable. Plato unequivocally and stridently asserts that the poet, i.e. the lyricist, the dramatist and the epic writer, writes when 'he is possessed and out of his mind, and his *reason* is no longer in him.' (1972: 43, emphasis added)

Plato's idea that reason and imagination, the rational faculty and the creative faculty do not keep company recurs throughout Western criticism. Philip Sidney in the Renaissance, P.B. Shelley in the Romantic age and, surprisingly enough, I.A. Richards in the twentieth century banish reason from literary creation and thereby fall in line with Plato. The most interesting case is that of Richards. Even though talking of mental adjustment that comes out of the enjoyment of poetry, he denies logic to the poetic universe and the language of poetry. He comes close to Derrida when he states:

> A poet may distort his statements; he may make statements which have logically nothing to do with the subject under treatment; he may, by metaphor and otherwise, present objects for thought which are logically quite irrelevant, he may perpetrate *logical non-sense*, be as trivial or as silly, logically, as it is possible to be. (180–81, emphasis added)

This is the kind of approach to literature which supports Derrida's untenable beliefs. But tradition to which Richards belongs has been rejected in favour of the alternative tradition which assimilates reason and imagination in artistic creation and which includes eminent critics like Aristotle, Horace, Dryden, Johnson, Coleridge, Wordsworth, Arnold and Leavis. Modern critics with the exception of Richards have emphasized in varying degrees thought and logic in literature.

Here the two critics who stand out are Jon Crowe Ransom and Yvor Winters, who have been discussed at length in the following pages.

In the present work, Derrida's concept of language and literature has been rejected using as the springboard the alternative thinkers from Vološinov to Habermas and an alternative concept of language as well as literature rooted in culture and society has been evolved. Habermas has defended the identity of philosophy by separating it from literature. I have tried to establish the identity of literature by separating it from philosophy and other disciplines.

Notes

1. I.A. Richards first published his book in 1934 which was around the time the New Critics emerged. See *Coleridge on Imagination* (London: Routledge and Kegan Paul, 1968).
2. See *Blindness and Insight* (New York: Oxford University Press, 1971) p. 28. Both Coleridge and the New Critics are organic thinkers who set great store by organic unit which is a red rag to Derrida and his followers who have unqualified faith in disjunction, decentring and dissemination.

Works Cited

Derrida, Jacques. *Acts of Literature,* ed. Derek Attridge. London: Rutledge, 1991.

Eichenbanm, Boris. 'The Theory of the Formal Method.' *Russian Formalist Criticism,* ed. L.T. Lemon and Marion J. Reiss. Lincoln. Nebr.: University of Nembraska Press, 1965.

Habermas, Jürgen. 'Leveling the Genre Distinction between Philosophy and Literature.' *The Derrida-Habermas Reader,* ed.

Lasse Thomassen. Edinburgh: Edinburgh University Press, 2006.

Krieger, Murray. 'Literature versus *Écriture:* Constructions and Deconstructions in Recent Critical Theory.' *Contemporary Criticism,* ed V.S. Seturaman. Madras: Macmillan India, 1989.

Mikics, David. *Who was Jacques Derrida?* New Haven: Yale University Press, 2009.

Plato. *Ion. Ancient Literary Criticism,* ed. D.A. Russell and M. Winterbotton. London: Oxford University Press, 1972

——. *The Republic,* trans. Desmond Lee. Harmonds. Worth: Penguin Books, 1974.

Richards, I.A. *Practical Criticism.* New York: Harcourt Brace Jovanovich, 1929.

Ricoeur, Paul, *The Rule of Metaphor,* trans. Robert Czerny. London: Rutledge and Kegan Paul, 1978.

CHAPTER 2

Humanism, Deconstruction, and Literature

The present chapter seeks to examine what the humanist critics have to say in order to salvage literature with its distinct identity. I single out four humanists known for their scholarly and critical achievements, namely Cleanth Brooks, Murray Krieger, M.H. Abrams and Helen Gardner.

Humanists and deconstructionists have been at loggerheads ever since Derrida emerged on the scene, which reminds one, albeit in a somewhat different form and context, the old conflict between philosophers and poets going back to Plato and Aristotle. When all is said and done, the deconstructionist are at bottom of philosophers, if not by training, then certainly in critical attitude and performance, who have usurped the territory literature. Humanists, on the other hand, have fought a fierce, though losing, battle on behalf of literature to prevent its merger with philosophy. While one admires their sincere efforts to save literature from the onslaught of deconstruction, one feels at the same time that they are answering the enemies of literature from outside targeting their edifice without destroying the foundation on which it stands. All four humanists have full faith in the New Critical postulate that literature exists as distinct from non-literature and believe with minor variations that literature has human concerns. And naturally, therefore, they feel greatly challenged by the poststructuralist demolition of their beliefs and certitudes. In this distressful situation they reiterate their long held convictions and reassert their faith in literature's human concerns, but, except for M.H. Abrams, they do not grapple with the problems of language wherein lies the basic issue.

Cleanth Brooks invokes Rene' Wellek, M.H. Abrams and E.D. Hirsch who are on his side in the defence of literature. In the two citations that Brooks gives from Wellek, the latter gives a common sense reply to what he designates 'the prophets of the death of literature'. In the first citation Wellek argues that certain literary devices which have played a pivoted role in the formation of literature, such as motifs, themes, images and symbols, are only marginally related to language. Moreover, great writers like Homer, Dante, Shakespeare and Tolstoy have been available in translations which have been greatly enjoyed and appreciated, although they convey very little of the peculiarities of their authors' language. This goes to prove, opines Wellek, that literature exists to a great extent independently of its linguistic form. In the second citation, Wellek answers those who maintain that man is imprisoned in language:

> We must assume that language itself is in an ontological relation to reality, as all older philosophers of language and even Heidegger assert. There is, after all, a perceptual life of man: personality and self ... cannot be reduced to language

relations. Even deaf-mutes find their way around the world. (Qtd. in Brooks, 491)

Brooks reckons Wellek's argument a powerful refutation of all that structuralism and poststructuralism say about language and literature. Wellek is a redoubtable scholar in the domain of literary theory and criticism but his reply is from outside the real battle over language and literature. He has every right to hold on to his own beliefs just as his opponents can hold on to their own. Conventional and contemporary critics stay safe within their own bounds.

Brooks next turns to M.H. Abrams, who is known for his humanism and extraordinary scholarship, and his wide-ranging interest in theory is evident from books like *The Mirror and the Lamp* and *A Glossary of Literary Terms.* There is no doubt that of Brook's trio, Abrams puts up the toughest fight to save literature with all its human concerns. Unfortunately, the two citations that Brooks gives from Abrams are not the best that one can glean from Abrams's extensive writings. In the first quotation, Abrams tells us how in recent criticism a work of literature is gratuitously reduced to text and literature to *écriture* which is writing in general. Abrams is apparently unhappy about this reductionism, as he believes in an independent identity of literature with human concern. In the second quotation, Abrams addresses another problem in contemporary theory, which relates to language. According to these recent theorists, language does not work in the conventional sense, as it does not communicate any determinate meaning. As Brooks points out, Abrams challenges this assumption and demonstres how language works in actual practice, as he can successfully 'warn somebody to get out of the way of a rushing truck.' (Qtd. in Brooks, 492)

One does agree with the points made by Abrams but at the same time one feels that his arguments are based on mere common sense. The arguments of his opponents are backed by a theory of language and in order to answer them, one has first to evolve an alternative theory of language which Abrams does not.

The third critic whom Brooks invokes in his support is E.D. Hirsch known for his Hermeneutics. In the extract that Brooks cites, Hirsch makes general observations on the problem in contemporary theory. Instead of focusing on the nature and function of literature, argues Hirsch, they focus on the nature and function of language. Fair enough, but instead of marshalling his arguments to refute these theorists' view of language, he simply asks a rhetorical question: 'Is language (mind you *language*, not merely poems) self-referential?' (Qtd. in Brooks, 429) Brooks gives another quotation from Hirsch wherein he advises critics to stay away from the anti-humanistic discourses of contemporary critics and return to what they can do best, which is to understand and help others understand the discourses of literature'. (Qtd. in Brooks, 494–95) This is again a common sense response to the challenge posed by the theorists Hirsch is fighting against. Hirsch presumes that literature exists notwithstanding what the recent theorists say to the contrary.

Having garnered support from others, Brooks formulates his own critical position which is succinctly expressed in the following statements:

> Literature tells the *truth*, but, as Emily Dickinson says in one of her poems, it tells it at a 'slant.' It tells the truth through a *fiction,* but it is the truth nonetheless. Literature has something to say about *reality* and is in fact one of the clearest available windows for looking out on to reality. (498)

> I want to return finally to the issue of the *referentiality* of literature—to the claim that, in spite its understanding of the use of fiction and analogy, literature nevertheless provides us with *knowledge.* (499)

There are four terms here—truth, reality, referentiality and knowledge—which are foregrounded with the implicit intention of demolishing the poststructuralist rejection of these very ideas. One appreciates Brook's intention but the mere assertion of these certitudes without taking cognizance of the arguments advanced by the opponents will not take us very far. Truth and knowledge are predicated on the referentiality of language and, therefore, in order to assert their presence in literature, we must first establish with plausible arguments that language is referential. It is true that throughout the essay, from which the above quotations come, Brooks inveighs against the poststructuralists, but this is done without going to the heart of the matter which is embedded in language.

Murray Krieger, a well-known critic with sympathies for the New Criticism, takes up cudgels against contemporary critics to save literature from possible extinction. At one place in his essay on 'Literature Versus *Écriture*: Constructions and Deconstructions in Recent Critical Theory', he speaks of our 'common sense awareness' and the essay, though full of critical insights and perceptive observations, is very much a common sense approach to the problems of language and literature. Krieger tells us repeatedly what literature, particularly poetry, has always been and how it has withstood the onslaught of recent theories. After a brief survey of contemporary theories, such as the Geneva school, reader-response criticism and structuralism, Krieger locks horns with the deconstructionists, especially Paul de Man. Although differing with them on several counts, he does not reject Deconstruction altogether but tries to assimilate it to his own theory.

For Krieger, Saussure's structural linguistics does not permit any privileging of literary discourse, which like any other discourse, is *parole*, an individual manifestation of the universal *langue*. This basic concept of Saussure's linguistics is adopted and adapted by both the structuralists and the poststructuralists who, writes Krieger, 'represent history's egalitarian revenge upon the New Criticism's aristocratic worship of the poem as a privileged and hence élite object.' (529) Fredric Jameson's 'prisonhouse of language', to which René Wellek refers, and Edward Said's 'the communal sea of linguisity', which is drawn on by Abrams, are replaced in Krieger's essay by 'Barthes's sea of *écriture*' into which is lost the unique identity of literature. René Wellek, M.H. Abrams as well as Murray Krieger jettison the metaphors employed by these recent critics to delineate what takes place in recent theories.

Krieger asks several rhetorical questions to express the agony that he feels in the midst of the common 'sea of *écriture*':

> How, then, can I at this late date urge the deviationist claim for poetry which I need if I am to urge its separatist mode of functioning? For how—to ask the same question another way—can I still speak of 'normal' discourse as a mythical background against which deviations are to occur? Can recent arguments for a seamless *écriture* altogether wipe out our *common sense awareness* of the distinction between those discourses which are predicated on the assumption that they are telling us about a 'reality' outside

> language—that they are more or less 'true'—and those which are self-consciously cultivated fictions. (534, emphasis added)

The main flaw in Krieger's reply to the recent theorists, particularly the deconstructionists, is suggested by the phrase 'common sense awareness'. Krieger is in the midst of the critics who complicate and problematize all common place assumptions and hence a reply to them in terms of common sense will not do. All those who care for literature will lend credence to Krieger's conclusions, but we cannot arrive at them without rejecting with plausible arguments the basic premises of the masters of structuralism and poststructuralism regarding language. The positive side of Krieger's arguments, drawing as it does on sheer common sense, is not strong enough to disturb the enemies of literature.

In another case of his common sense approach, Krieger distinguishes between the discourse which aims at communicating 'extralinguistic notions' and the literary discourse which exploits the 'internalized play of its verbal medium' in order to produce meaning. This distinction is denied by Derrida and his acolytes who believe that whatever characteristics you discern in literary discourse are also present in discourse which we consider non-literary. In order to rebut this claim of the deconstructionists, Krieger writes:

> I argue, then, that most trained readers of poetry feel an acute difference between discourse characterized by a self-generating play of words which maximally exploits all that is potentially in them, exploding them into its meaning and the loosely instrumental 'use' of words selected from the bag of almost equal candidates for service which our culture places at our disposal to carry—one or another of

> them in its minimal way—a predetermined extralinguistic meaning. (535)

This is a clear and a concise distinction between literature and non-literature. It is true that literature exploits language to its maximal potential, which is not true of non-literature but the deconstructionists will be quick to reply that this distinction is untenable and demonstrate with great ingenuity how words function outside literature precisely as they do in literature. However, we do know and feel the distinction that Krieger makes. But this distinction needs to be systematically argued with definite views on the nature of language, which will necessitate a debate with linguists and the philosophers of language. When there is so much heated debate, we cannot go by feeling and common sense.

Although pleading for literature as a deviation from 'a neutral, normal discourse', Krieger is also inclined to accept deconstruction as far as possible. He comes dangerously close to his opponents when he writes:

> Modern theorists may be anxious to undercut the privilege granted to literature by leveling it into common *écriture*, but what they have for the most part done is to raise *écriture* (or at leaste those non-literary examples of *écriture* they are dealing with) into literature. If these critics argue against the exclusiveness of poetry (that is, fictions, 'imaginative literature') as the proper subject for criticism, and rather seek to include a wide range of works by essayists, philosophers and even social scientists, they do so by treating these works as texs to which techniques appropriate to literary criticism may be applied. Even more, their techniques of deconstruction, of 'unmetaphoring' their texts, are to a great extent echoes of what poems have

> always been doing to themselves and teaching their critics to do to them. It is for this reason I suggest that, instead of the concept of literature being deconstructed into *écriture, écriture* has been *consturcted* into literature. (539)

How do we react to this passage? Yes, in a sense deconstruction is the victory of literature over other disciplines, which have been transformed into literature, bringing into being a kind of literary empire. Literature is now ubiquitous but this very ubiquity takes away the unique identity of literature, which gives it a pride of place among the humanities and social sciences. The deconstructionists will be only too glad to lend credence to Krieger's arguments. A shrewd and talented critic like Krieger has fallen into the deconstructionist trap. To say, as Krieger does in the above citation, that the 'techniques of deconstruction ... are, to a great extent echoes of what poems have always been doing' is to go at least half the distance with the deconstructionists. If Deconstruction is only an extension of the techniques of poetry, then there is a reason for literary critics to feel jubilant over the vast empire that literature has now built. On the contrary, critics are worried and rightly so, over the dissolution of the boundary between literature and non-literature and the resultant death of literature. In the following extracts from *Dissemination*, Derrida himself wonders why the term 'literature' is still being used, as deconstruction has annihilated literature with a distinct identity:

> ... why is 'literature' still the name for that which already withdraws itself from what has always been conceived and signified by this name—or, not only eluding it, implacably destroys it. (Qtd in Bas, 341)

> Literature annihilates itself through its illimitability. (ibid.)

In view of the opinion expressed by Derrida in these quotations, Krieger's stand will have little justification. If literature has no limits, it loses its identity. If the term literature is still being used or some kind of writing is still viewed as literature, it only proves that the deconstructive destruction of literature is only an academic exercise.

In his systematic critique of deconstruction, M.H. Abrams, who is a strident advocate of Humanism, directs his attention to the linguistic premises of deconstruction in order to establish that Derrida's denial of reference is more apparent than real, as he does accept it by the backdoor. However, he does not address issues in linguistics and philosophy of language, which provide the foundation for Derrida's radical philosophy and criticism. Although he does not use the word 'common sense,' his approach to language and literature is based on his experience, as is evident from the following statement:

> An enquirer ... whose stand is in the world of human relations and interactions takes language to be a very complex set of shared practices and, upon investigating these practices, finds that we often manage very well to say what we mean and understand what someone else has undertaken to say. (Abrams, 1996: 14)

This is a recurring idea in Abrams's writings. In 'How to do Things with Texts' he speaks of an alternative to the Nietzschean/Derridean view of language:

> The alternative sets out from the observation that in practice language often works, that it gets its job done. We live a life in which we have assurance that we are able to mean what we say and know what we mean and in which

> our auditors or readers show us by their verbal and actional responses whether or not they have understood us correctly. (Abrams, 1979: 454)

This is a response to language in the light of empirical experience which disproves all that is said in abstract terms in the philosophical and critical speculations of Derrida. In fact, it is this common sense approach to language that Abrams uses as a springboard to demonstrate a discrepancy in Derrida's thinking, a contradiction between what he professes and what he practices.

The main thrust of Abrams's debate with Derrida is that the latter's deconstructive reading of a text is preceded by its conventional reading which makes use of reference. Abrams compares Derrida with David Hume, who lived a double life, a real life in which he shared beliefs and values with others in society and an intellectual life as a philosopher, which questioned these very beliefs and values. Similarly, Derrida forcefully denies conventional reading in his theory, but in actual practice quietly accepts it in order to construct the text before it is deconstructed. Abrams takes for example Derrida's extended reading of Rousseau's *Essay on the Origin of Language* which he subjects to both conventional and deconstructive readings:

> Derrida's double reading, reading 1 and reading 2, in fact produces two texts. One is the text such as Rousseau's *Essay* which he reads by accepting, in a provisional way, the standard conventions and legalities that establish as its boundaries the opening and closing lines of the printed form. Text 2 is produced by a sort of overrun that spoils all these boundaries and divisions .... (Abrams, 1986: 205)

What Abrams's reading of Derrida demonstrates is the indispensability of referential meaning on which depends Derrida's primary or conventional reading which engenders what Abrams calls text 1. However provisional this reading may be, it is there as the foundation for the deconstructive reading which spawns text 2.

Abrams discerns a similar acceptance of referentiality in the writings of Paul de Man and J. Hillis Miller. In both these critics, reference and rhetoric go side by side resulting in a double reading of texts. Both adopt a highly predictable procedure. They first use the referential meaning in order to construe the text and then adopt the deconstructive method to subvert this meaning. Commenting upon stage one of Hillis Miller's procedure, Abrams writes:

> I shall hazard a prediction as to what will Miller do then. He will have determinate things to say and will masterfully exploit the resources of language to express these things clearly and forcibly, addressing himself to us in the confidence that we, to the degree that we have mastered the constitutive norms of this kind of discourse, will approximate what he means. (Abrams, 1997: 447)

Abrams is right that this is reading the text the conventional way. But Miller's reading process does not stop here, as it is followed by stage two of his reading, which deconstructs the construction of stage one. The bottom line of Abrams's arguments is that reference is an integral part of deconstruction.

Not only does Abrams point out the use of reference in deconstructive analyses, he also demonstrates the presence in Derrida's writings of the reference-generated values which his theory apparently rejects such as truth and rightness. In his 'What is a Humanistic Criticism?' Abrams cites a statement by Derrida, which is his reply to Jürgen Habermas: 'This is false as opposed to true, and I defy Hebermas to prove the presence in my work of that 'primacy' of rhetoric which he attributes to me.' (Abrams, 1996: 18) Abrams gives another example where Derrida goes against his own theory. When Derrida launches an attack on the South African apartheid, he has no option but to accept the possibility of a determinate meaning in this context: 'There is no stability that is absolute, eternal, intangible, natural etc., [yet] I can consider the context of [a] discussion, like that of this one, to be very stable and very determined.' (ibid., 19) Derrida adds that his arguments leave open the possibilities of other interpretations, but this has never been denied by others who do not fall into his camp. Abrams has successfully established the presence in Derrida's writings of the referential property of language and the acceptance, however grudging, of the norms and values which go with reference. But as students of literature, our overriding concern is not so much the presence or absence of referentiality in language (which is certainly important for all of us) as the identity of literature. What has Abrams to say about it?

In his 'Construing and Deconstructing' Abrams states that the main problem for traditional critics who believe in the identity of literature is the 'claim that it is impossible even to identify anything called literature by establishing boundaries or specifying features, which set it off from other forms of writing.' (Abrams, 1986: 194) The claim in question, as we known, has been made by the poststructuralists. There is no doubt that Abrams is a very serious and perceptive student of literature but, reading the four essays to which references have been made, one gets the impression that he is much more concerned with the nature of language than with the nature of literature. Of course, the two are intertwined, especially in contemporary theories, but nevertheless the two are not the same. We need to identify and foreground those specific features of literature which mark it off from non-literature.

In her 'Present Discontents', Helen Gardner, like traditional humanists, takes up cudgels for literature and highlights the contribution it makes towards the understanding of human nature and conduct as well as human sensibility. She dismisses outright recent theories which she indignantly describes as 'perverse and barren exercise in ingenuity' giving one the impression of 'frivolity and triviality.' Unfortunately, there is more anger in her essay than cool thinking which is called for to take on a complex thinker like Derrida. Of course, any serious student of literature, who has enjoyed reading and discussing the great monuments of literary creation, will appreciate her defence of literature, but the arguments that she advances are the outcome of her common sense response to the challenge from contemporary theory:

> ... it is of course perfectly true that the author is not present in the flesh, as we read his book, for us to interrogate him. Even if he were, interrogation might not yield any very satisfying results ... . But to extend these truisms to deny that we are conscious as we read a book or a poem that we are reading the expression of an individual mind and sensibility, and that this is conveyed to us by an individual manner of expression that, like a voice, belongs to one person, would only be sense, if we were prepared to deny

> the possibility of any communication of mind with mind by the medium of the written word. (509)

This is, no doubt, solid common sense, but it does not take account of the process through which contemporary theorists, particularly deconstructionists arrive at their conclusion. The conclusion may be untenable, but the process needs to be examined. In Gardner's essay, there are several references to Neitzsche, who exercised a decisive impact on the deconstructionists, but Nietzsche's philosophical concepts and his concept of language are so interlocked that the they cannot be viewed separately. This is also true of the deconstructionists who are deeply rooted in linguistics and the philosophy of language. In order to answer the challenge posed by them, we cannot restrict ourselves to the surface but need to delve deep into the sources which lend substance and support to their theoretical positions. It is somewhat naive to compare, as Gardner does, the deconstructive impulse with the destructive urge of a child who 'with a glee knocks down a pile of bricks which his playmate has with great pains built up into a house'. (506) Whatever else the deconstructionists may be, they are by no accounts playful and immature children compared with serious and mature traditionalists like Gardner herself.

It must be said to the credit of the traditionalists that the four critics that we have discussed have made major contributions to literary studies. Their understanding of the nature and function of literature is beyond doubt. However, their critique of deconstruction is in the nature of a tangential argument, which neither demolishes deconstruction nor tells us comprehensively and precisely those qualities which are predominantly, if not exclusively, present in literature. Their diatribe against this very complex movement fails to shake its foundation. This is not to dismiss their critique which has its own relevance if only because it lends support to literature in its fight against deconstruction for survival.

Works Cited

Abrams, M.H. 'Construing and Deconstructing' (1986). *Essays in Modern Criticism*, ed. Rajnath & William I. Elliott. Delhi: Doaba Book House, 2006.

Abrams, M.H. 'How to Do Things with Texts' (1979). *Contemporary Criticism,* ed. V.S. Seturaman. Calcutta: Macmillan India, 1989.

Abrams, M.H. 'The Deconstructive Angel' (1977). *Contemporary Criticism*, ed. V.S. Seturaman. Calcutta: Macmillam India, 1989.

Abrams, M.H. 'What is a Humanistic Criticism?' *Journal of Literary Criticism,* Vol. VIII, No. 2 (December) 1996.

Bas, Alan. "'Literature'/Literature". *Velocities of Change*, ed. Richard Macksey. Baltimore: The Johns Hopkins University Press, 1974.

Brooks, Cleanth. 'The Primacy of the Linguistic Medium' (1986). *Contemporary Criticism,* ed. V.S. Seturaman. Calcutta: Macmillan India, 1989.

CHAPTER 3

Saussure, Language and Literature—I

As is now common knowledge in the domain of criticism and theory, Derrida denies to literature any exclusive properties. To him, what is in literature is also discernible outside literature in any discipline which makes use of language as a medium resulting in the inevitable conclusion that language as such is literature. This not only effaces the identity of literature but brings disciplines generally reckoned non-literary like philosophy, linguistics, history, etc. within the orbit of literary discourse. Jûrgen Habermas, the German philosopher, has salvaged the identity of philosophy by demonstrating the difference between it and literature[1]. But a similar attempt ought to be made from the side of literature to save its identity.

Derrida has built up his theory on the foundation provided by Saussure's linguistics which views language as non-referential and differential. This has been used by Derrida and his acolytes to demolish the conventional concept of literature as mimesis or representation. When language does not refer to reality, how can literature imitate or reflect it? But language has been viewed differentially by different linguists and philosophers of language, and if Saussure's theory of language is replaced by another theory, then we shall have a different concept of literature. Saussure's theory became available to us only in 1916 when his students put together their classroom notes in a book form under the title *Course in General Linguists.* But fresh developments have taken place in the study of language since 1916 which can be used as a springboard to argue that literature does exist with an independent identity and that it represents reality. Bakhtin and his circle situate language in society, Edward Sapir believes that language is a product of culture, Benjamin Lee Whorf is of the opinion that one's worldview is determined by one's linguistic background and Austin and Searle's speech act theory sets great store by context which exists not in the abstract linguistic system but in the real world in which people live and communicate.

Bakhtin's monumental achievement was recognized late but he can be looked upon as a central figure in Russian literary criticism, who challenged Saussure long before he became known in other countries. What a coincidence that the two Russians who exercised tremendous influence on later linguistic and critical speculations were moving at the same time in opposite directions in their approaches to language. Making use of the Saussurean linguistics in his own writings, Roman Jakobson, a Russian formalist, became instrumental in introducing it to France and America. Moving in the opposite direction, Bakhtin questions the formalism of Saussure's linguistics and setting himself in opposition to it sets forth his own version of linguistics and poetics with sociological dimension.

Language for Bakhtin and his circle, which included V.N. Vološinov and P.N. Medvedev, is not only situated in society but also imbued with ideology. In his 'Discourse in the Novel', Bakhtin avers that he takes 'language not as a system of abstract grammatical categories, but rather language conceived as ideologically situated' (354). As against Saussure who believes that all languages can be studied by the same norms and rules and, thus, reduces them to a single language, Bakhtin holds that even a single language takes on multiple forms in the actual speeches of persons depending on the profession and social groups to which they belong. For Saussure, reality is constructed by language but for Bakhtin language is rooted in social reaiity which shapes and develops it. He wants the linguist to concern himself with the language as it exists in socieity with all its multiplicity and variety. The reduction of multiple languages to a single unitary language in Saussure's linguistic system is untenable to him. His glorification of the novel and denigration of the epic and the lyric is a direct outcome of his attitude towards language. He rejects the stylistic analysis of the novel done in the light of Saussure's linguistics, which substitutes the single language of the novelist for the multiple languages of the novel or isolates for analysis unitary features of the poetic genres such as 'image, symbol, poetic language', etc.:

> Equally in both cases, style is understood in the spirit of Saussure as an individualization of the general language .... The whole of the novel and specific tasks involved in constructing this whole out of heteroglot, multivoiced,

> multistyled, and often multilanguaged elements remain outside the boundaries of such a study. (264–65)

It is the language of the novel which comes close to the language of the people as it is actually spoken. But the stylistic analyses based on Saussure's linguistics fail to do full justice to the genre of the novel, as it reduces its inherent multivoicedness to the single voice of the poetic genres.

If Bakhtin goes against Saussure in accepting as his norm the living speech of the people, V.N. Vološino, an important member of the Bakhtin circle, rejects Saussure's linguistics out of hand in his *Marxism and the Philosophy of Language* published as early as 1929. In the chapter on 'Language, Speech, and Utterance', he raises as many as eight objections to Saussure's linguistics. The following are the four main reservations:

1. It is not possible to separate the synchronic system of language from its diachronic counterpart. Language is not static, but dynamic and flows continuously from the past to the present into the future. In this current of language it is not possible to identify a static moment which can be studied synchronically: 'there is no real moment in time when a synchronic system of language could be constructed' (66).

2. One cannot divorce system from speech, as the two constitute an indivisible unit. Language exists in society for verbal communication between human beings who exist in time, and by 'viewing living language as if it were dead and alien abstract objectivism makes language something external to the stream of verbal communication.' (81)

3. Saussure ignores context in which language makes sense. He does not realize that the same word has different meanings in different contexts: 'there are as many meanings of a word as there are contexts of its usage.' (79).

4. Linguistic signs are not arbitrarily related to their meanings, as they come charged with ideology and become 'an arena of class struggle.'(23) 'The divorce of language from its ideological impletion,' writes Vološinov 'is one of abstract objectivism's most serious errors.' (71)

As is evident from these objections, Vološinov places himself at the other extreme from Saussure. In his linguistic speculations, he underlines individuality and subjectivism in the study of language as against the collectivism and objectivism of Saussure. Saussure looks upon language, argues Volosinov, not as living and creative but as dead and inert: 'Language as readymade product, as a stable system, is, so to speak, the inert crust, the hardened lava of language creativity.' (48) Throughout the chapter on 'Two Trends of Thought', Vološinov launches a broadside at Saussure and his synchronic linguistics which he dismisses as 'abstract objectivism.' At the end of the chapter, he ask a rhetorical question:

> What then is the true centre of linguistic reality: the individual speech act—the utterance—or the system of language? And what is the mode of existence of language: unceasing creative generation or inert mutability of self-identical norm? (63)

We know on which side of the divide stands Vološinov. He wants language to be treated as a living and creative entity and to this effect the emphasis has to be shifted to speech and utterance which are marginalized in Saussure's linguistics.

Edward Sapir, who has been widely acclaimed for his contribution to anthropology, psychology and linguistics, views language as a product of culture and society. In his essay on 'The status of linguistics as a Science', published as far back as 1929, Sapir affirms: 'language is primarily a cultural or social product and must be understood as such.' (76) He postulates a reciprocal relation between language and culture as well as society. Language comes out of culture and society and in turn contributes to our understanding of them. 'Language is a guide to social reality,' writes Sapir and he goes on to say:

> The 'real world' is to a large extent unconsciously built up on the language habits of the groups. No two languages are sufficiently similar to be considered as representing the same social reality. (69)

Language for Sapir plays the pivotal role in social and cultural formations. This kind of give-and-take between language and society is beyond the purview of Saussure's linguistics which views language as self-referential and as such detached from reality.

In his essay on 'Language', published in 1933, Sapir further distances himself from the Saussurean linguistics. That Saussure and Sapir are at the opposite extremes is evidenced by the following extracts:

> A further psychological character of language is the fact that while it may be looked upon as a symbolic system which reports or refers to or otherwise substitutes for direct experience, it does not as a matter of actual behaviour stand

> apart from or run parallel to direct experience but completely interpenetrates with it. (8)

> On our own level it is generally difficult to make a complete divorce between objective reality and our linguistic symbols of reference to it and things, qualities, and events are on the whole felt to be what they are called. (8–9)

Between these two citations Sapir has made it clear that linguistic symbols (which are synonymous with Saussure's signs) not only refer to external reality but also interpenetrate it. Language and reality, says Sapir, cannot be divorced as they act and interact upon each other and coalesce.

Taking his cue from Sapir, Whorf expounds his theory that the world view of a people is constructed by their language habits. Whereas Sapir discerns a reciprocal relation between language and culture, Whorf concerns himself solely with the impact of language on our thinking. In one of his seminal essays, 'The Relation of Habitual Thought and Behaviour to Language' (1939), Whorf begins with a long epigraph from Sapir, which includes the following:

> Human beings do not live in the objective world alone, nor alone in the world of social activity as ordinarily understood, but are very much at the mercy of the particular language which has become the medium of expression for their society ... . We see and hear and otherwise experience very largely as we do because the language habits of our community predispose certain choices of interpretation. (134)

What is not clear from this quotation is that for Sapir, language is also a product of culture and society. The reciprocal relationship between language and the external world that Sapir postulates is absent from Whorf's thinking. However, both the thinkers believe that language and reality are interrelated.

With the help and guidance of Sapir, Whorf makes an extended study of Hopi, the language spoken by the Hopi, a group of native Americans, demonstrates how the worldview of the Hopi is an outcome of the structure of their language. For example, the Hopi's concept of time and space is different from that of the Europeans and the difference is due to the difference in grammar and language. Unlike the Europeans, they have no idea of time as a 'smooth flowing continuum' in which everything is constantly moving and changing. Distinguisting the Hopi's concept of time from that of the Europeans, Whorf writes:

> To us, for whom time is a motion on a space, unvarying repetition seems to scatter its force along a row of units of that space and be wasted. To the Hopi, for whom time is not a motion but a 'getting later' of everything that has ever been done, unvarying repetition is not wasted but accumulated ... it is as if the return of the day were felt as the return of the same person, a little older but with all the impresses of yesterday, not as 'another day', i.e. like an entirely different person. (151)

The Hopi view the length of time not in terms of change but in terms of accumulation. Instead of saying that 'they stayed ten days' they say 'they stayed until the eleventh day.' Whorf believes that the Hopi's way of measuring time not as 'a relation between two events in lateness' but as becoming later' is more rational.

Like Bakhtin and his circle's theory of language, the Sapir-Whorf thesis undermines the argument of Saussure that language is divorced from reality. This language controversy of the twentieth century reminds one of a similar controversy over the world-object relation (which is akin to the signifier-signified relation in Saussure's linguistics) that took place in ancient India. In his significantly titled book, *The Word and the World*, Bimal Krishna Matilal gives an account of this controversy: Whereas the Nyaya-Vaisesika School holds that the word-object relation is created by man-made convention, the grammarians and the Mimamsakas believe that the relation is natural and eternal. The former argue that the word and the object belong to different realms and, therefore, their connection can be only man-made. The word 'pot', for example, which is a group of three letters, is located in speech, whereas the object 'pot', which we recognize when the word is uttered, is a physical entity on the floor. These two separate entities can be brought together only by convention which is created by men.

The grammarians and the Mimamsakas who plead for the eternal, i.e. natural and non-arbitrary relation between the word and the object marshal the following arguments:

1. It is the form of the material object, not the object such as a pot which is implied by the word. An individual object is destructible and also variable (there are many kinds of pot) but the form of the object survives for ever.

2. If the relation between the word and the object is an outcome of convention, then the question arises as to who created this convention. Who was the first person who called the object 'pot' pot.

3. When the child learns his language from his parents, he does not establish connections between words and objects but only recognizes the connections already established.

It is clear from the controversy between the two groups of Indian thinkers that more than one approach to language is possible and we can choose the one which is the more convincing and which suits our purpose. I find a lot of substance in the arguments of the grammarians and the Mimamsakas that the word-object relation is natural and essential.[2] After all, if we take any language at a particular stage of its development, we shall find that words are taken as referential not because they refer to any particular objects but they refer to what Indian thinkers have called the forms of objects. Matilal is dead right when he says:

> It is not improbable to conceive that at different periods in the history of the development of a language, there was a consensus regarding the use of certain words to denote certain objects and convey certain meanings. (29)

This view of language flies in the face of the deconstructive theory of language where words (read signs) are non-referential and meanings always uncertain.[3]

Drawing on Mikhail Bakhtin and his circle, Carl Sanders Peirce and Hilary Putnam, S.P. Mohanty arives at the conclusion that the sign and its meaning are embedded in culture and society. For reason best known to him, he does not use the findings of Sapir and Whorf who have expressed views similar to his. His main target is Paul de Man, not, surprisingly, his mentor Jacques Derrida. De Man, according to him, does not believe in the epistemic dimension of language which he dissociates completely from the circumambient reality. 'The problem with de Man's view of language,' he writes, 'is that it proceeds a little too hastily from a rejection of crude notion of reference as a guarantee of meaning to an implausible theory of language as essentially figural, defined by the indeterminable rhetorical play that subverts the security of any meaning.'(34) Mohanty dismisses this view and sets himself in opposition to all those who hold similar views. He believes in an alternative theory which relates sign to society and culture. Like others settled in the metropolitan West, Gayatri Spivak and Homi Bhabha, for example, Mohanty does not turn to Indian theories of language and meaning to garner support for his view.

There is no denying that deconstruction rejects reference and postulates the impossibilities of conveying any determinate meaning which constitutes the core of logic or truth. Against this concept of language, Mohanty sets his own view, derived from several Western thinkers, which relates language to society:

> I argue implicitly that we can begin to understand the productivity of language and signification only when we have a better account of reference which explains the *variety* of (causal) relations between language and the world and, in particular, between signs and their social contexts. (35)

This view certainly finds support in Bakhtin, Pierce, and Putnam, the sources that Mohanty has tapped but this also bears a close resemblance to the opinions expressed by Sapir and Whorf as well as Indian thinkers ignored by Mohanty. Interestingly enough, Edward Said, who is better grounded in Western theories than Indian thinkers, turns to Arabic linguistics for support to his view of language and reality. In the titular essay of his book, *The World, the Text and the Critic,* Said observes how contemporary speculations about language in Europe were anticipated in the eleventh century by Islamic philosophic grammarians. Of the too distinct approaches to language by these grammarians he writes:

> Batinists held that the meaning in language is concealed within the words, meaning is therefore available only as the result of an inward tending exegesis. The Zaharites—their names derive from the Arabic word for clear, apparent, and phenomenal; Batin connotes internal—argued that words had only a surface meaning, one that was anchored to a particular usage, circumstance, historical and religious situation. (36)

One can easily see the parallel between the two groups of Arab linguists and two groups of Indian linguists discussed above. The citation from Said suggests that the Saussure-type linguistics is not the only linguistic theory we can fall back upon. As we have noticed, even in ancient times, other options were available to students of literature and literary criticism. If we adopt an option which goes against Saussure, we shall have another view of literature. If by using Saussure's linguistics, Derrida can build up his esoteric theory which is detrimental to the identity of literature, an alternative theory which separates literature from other disciplines can be evolved by drawing on the findings of other linguists.

The relation between the signifier and the signified may or may not be arbitrary, but there is a difference between the two which is of great significance. The signifier does not change from person to person. Imagine 10 persons producing the sign or the sound 'dog'. They will write the sign or produce the sound differently, but these differences do not matter, as essentially they produce the same signifier and refer to the same animal. Each signifier has a fixed signified, but it can have any number of other signifieds, depending on the context in which it is used. Here I take the help of the *Oxford Advanced Learner's Dictionary*, 8th addition (2010). The entry on 'dog' first gives the fixed meaning of the sign as

> an animal with four legs and a tail, often kept as a pet or trained for work, for example hunting or guarding buildings.

After giving this invariant meaning, the dictionary refers the reader to the entries on guide dog, gun dog, hearing dog, lap dog, pairie dog, sheep dog, sniffer dog and tracker dog. Further, the dictionary provides idiomatic meanings of the sign 'dog' in expressions like a dog in the manger, 'a dog's breakfast/dinner,' 'a dog's life,' 'every dog has his day,' 'give a dog a bad name,' 'go to the dog,' 'not have a dog's chance,' 'why keep a dog and bark yourself?' For more idiomatic expressions, the reader is referred to the entries on hair, rain, sick, sleep, tail, and teach. Thus, the signifier 'dog' has multiple signifieds in different contexts, besides a fixed signified to which it is tied. The relation between the signifier and the fixed signified may be arbitrary, but the multiple signifieds of the signifier are determined by culture and society. This goes to prove that formalism is not enough. The sign is both a linguistic and a cultural unit. As a linguistic unit, it has a fixed meaning, but as a cultural unit it has variable meanings. Signs are used to communicate meaning and in order to communicate it fully and effectively, we need to fall back upon their linguistic as well as cultural and social dimensions. The referentiality of language needs to be restored for a meaningful communication. And once the referentiality is restored, Derrida's deconstructive approach to language will fall to pieces, and trace which, for Derrida, leads to erasure, difference, and finally aporia will be out of the question. It is by discerning aporia in all writings that Derrida dissolves the distinction between literature and non-literature.

Notes

1. Jürgen Habermas, 'Levelling The Genre Distinction between Philosophy and Literature,' *The Habermas- Derrida Reader,* ed. Lasse Thomassen (Edinburgh: Edinburgh University Press, 206), pp. 13–14.

2. This comes very close to Eco's opinion in his *A Theory of Semiotics* where he writes:

   Let us try to understand the nature of the object that corresponds to an expression. Take the term/dog/. The referent will certainly not be the dog X standing by me while I am pronouncing the word. For anyone who holds to the doctrine of the referent, the referent in such a case will be all existing dogs. But 'all existing dogs' is not an object which can be perceived with the senses. It is a set, a class .... (66–67)

3. What Matilal states is confirmed by Robert Scholes, the author of the first comprehensive account of structuralism in English, who questions the arbitrary nature of linguistic signs and argues that the relation between sound and object, i.e. signifier and signified in Saussure's linguistics is not arbitrary, in a particular culture:

   The connection between sound and concept is arbitrary with respect to nature, of course, but not to culture. We who grow up in English must call a tree a tree if we wish to be understood. (16)

Works Cited

Bakhtin, M.M. *The Dialogic Imagination,* ed. Michael Holquist, tr. Caryl Emerson. Austin: University of Texas Press, 1983.

Eco, Umberto. *A Theory of Semiotics.* Bloomington: Indiana University Press, 1976.

Matilal, Bimal Krishna. *The Word and the World.* New Delhi: Oxford University Press, 2001.

Mohanty, S.P. *Literary Theory and the Claims of History.* New Delhi: Oxford University Press, 1998.

Said, Edward. *The World, the Text and the Critic.* London: Vintage, 1991.

Sapir, Edward. *Culture, Language and Personality,* ed. David G. Mandelbaum. Berkley: University of California Press, 1949.

Scholes, Robert. *Struturalism in Literature.* New Haven: Yale University Press, 1974.

Saussure, Ferdinand de. *Course in General Linguistics,* tr. Wade Baskin. New York: McGraw-Hill Book Company, 1966.

Vološinov, V.N. *Marxism and the Philosophy of Language,* tr. Ladislav Matejka and J.R. Titunik. New York: Seminar Press, 1973.

Whorf, Benjamin Lee. *Language, Thought and Reality.* Cambridge, Mass.: The M.I.T. Press, 1979.

CHAPTER 4

Saussure, Language and Literature—II

Even accepting Saussure's idea that language is self-referential and differential, one may not necessarily go Derrida's way. Saussure is not against literature or literary language nor does he believe that culture in the conventional sense has come to an end. In chapter V of *Course in General Linguistics,* entitled 'Internal and External Elements of Language', Saussure takes a highly sensible position which differs radically from the extremely complicated and unduly problemtized position of Derrida. Saussure admits that external elements which influence the formation and growth of a language matter but all the same language can and should be studied formally, i.e. in terms of its internal construction. Of the two major influences, namely culture, of which ethnology forms a significant segment and politics, Saussure writes:

> The culture of a nation exerts an influence on its language, and the language, on the other hand, is largely responsible for the nation. (20)

> Great historical events like the Roman Conquest have an incalculable influence on a host of linguistic facts. Colonization, which is only one form that conquest may take, brings about changes in an idiom by transporting it into different surroundings. (20)

The first citation above brings Saussure close to the Sapir- Whorf thesis. But these ideas about language are alien to Derrida's thinking. However, Saussure and Derrida are at one that language is best studied internally. What matters in language is not the external influence but the internal construction which is shaped by the rules which go into the making of what Saussure calls *langue.*

While keeping his focus on *langue,* Saussure does not hesitate in talking about *parole,* which, being an individual manifestation of *langue,* includes literary creations. He makes a twofold division of *parole* into literary or book language and spoken language for which he has used two other terms, dialect and vernacular. Further, he envisages the possibility of an interaction between the two:

> At every point the literary language oversteps the boundaries that literature apparently marks off; we need only to consider the influence of *salons,* the court, and national academies. Moreover, the literary language raises the important question of conflicts between it and local dialects; the linguist must also examine the reciprocal relations of book language and the vernacular; for every literary language, being the product of the culture, finally breaks away from its natural sphere, the spoken language. (25)

The two manifestations of *langue* in the domain of *parole,* the literary language and spoken language, are intertwined in a give-and-take relationship. The spoken language can take the form of dialect at one extreme and the language spoken in the *salon*, the court and the national academic at the other. By the same logic the literary or book language can take more than one form. It can be divided as in Habermas, into the language of the humanities (other than literature) and social sciences and the language of literature. This possibility is not closed in Saussure's linguistics. There is no denying that the medium of literature is the same as that of day-to-day conversations, humanities, sciences and social sciences. Granted that language cannot be divided into exclusive categories, all the same there are enough differences between the language of literature and that of non-literature to mark them off from each other. Saussure is not averse to the idea of literature as distinct from non-literature. It all depends on how Saussure linguistics is used and what in it is made use of. Using it Derrida builds up a theory which is detrimental to the identity of literature. But using the same linguistics Roman Jakobson, Jürij Lotman and Jonathan Culler evolve their theories of literature and literary forms.

As far as my information goes, Jokobson was the first to make use of Saussure's linguistics in literary studies. As early as 1923, he published a book on Czech versification in which he took note of Saussure's linguistics. And in 1928, he published an essay in collaboration with Bogatyrev Pyotra Bogatynev in which Saussure's linguistics is used to build a theory for a more adequate study of folklore. Although using Saussure's linguistics as a springboard for his critical speculations, Jakobson nowhere denies the identity of literature. In an early book, *Modern Russian Poetry,* he writes: 'The object of the science of literature is not literature, but literariness—that is that which makes a given work a work of literature'(qtd in Eichenbaum,107). This is not Derrida's literariness which is ubiquitous, but the literariness of literary works. His later writings like 'Linguistics and Poetics' and 'Poetry of Grammar and Grammar of Poetry' reinforce the identity of literature. In fact, Jakobson is known as the father of stylistics which is the study of the language of literature. While this movement came into existence in Anglo-American Criticism in the 1950s, in Russian criticism this goes backs to the year 1916 when 'Society for the Study of the Language of Literature' was set up.

Jakobson's codes consisting of the six elements involved in all linguistic communications and the corresponding six functions have been formulated in order to identify and distinguish different linguistic formations, including literature. Jakobson, who has influenced Habermas's view of language, thinks in terms of predominance, not exclusiveness. He states clearly and categorically that in any linguistic communication, literary or non-literary, all the six elements operate, although only one of them predominates. Thus, in poetry, which is the most literary of literary forms, the focus is on message which for him is not meaning but utterance or speech. Describing the poetic function of language, Jakobson writes:

> Poetic function is not the sole function of verbal art, but only its dominant function whereas in all other verbal activities it acts as a subsidiary, accessory constituent. This function, by promoting the palpability of signs, deepens the fundamental dichotomy of signs and objects. (356)

The argument marshalled here dissipates the confusion spawned by Derrida who demands purity of language shorn of all traces of what Jakobson calls poetic function, and as no such language exists, he concludes that there is no difference between literature and non-literature.

Roman Jakobson, like the other Russian formalists, distinguishes not only between literature and non-literature but also between different literary genres. In his *Fundamentals of Language,* written in collaboration with Morris Hall, he draws on Saussure's linguistics to make the widely acclaimed and extensively used distinction between metaphor and metonymy. Relating two kinds of language disorders in children suffering from aphasia to the two rhetorical figures, metaphor and metonymy, which are respectively paradigmatic and syntagmatic in Saussure's terminology, Jakobson argues that the former is predominant in poetry and the latter in prose fiction. Moreover, if we think in terms of literary trends and movements, says Jakobson, then remanticism and symbolism are informed by the 'primacy of metaphoric process' whereas the realistic trend is predominantly metonymic.

Jakobson's poetics makes it clear that Saussure's linguistics is not opposed to the identity of literarature. Jakobson understands linguistics as well as literature much better than Derrida if only because he is a student of both linguistics and literature whereas the latter is only a philosopher by training. In fact, Jakobson stands like a colossus striding the two disciplines, and he has done more than anyone else to introduce Saussure's linguistics in the domain of literary criticism.

Besides Jakobson, Jürij Lotman in the Soviet Union and Janathan Culler in the United States have evolved their theories of literature by drawing on Saussure's linguistics. Lotman published his major works over a period of less than a decade between 1964 and 1973, the most important of them being *The Structure of The Artistic Text* published in 1970 and translated into English in 1977. Resting his speculations on Saussure's linguistics, particularly his ideas of system, paradigmatics and syntmatics, he makes a threefold division of Saussure's *parole* into the language of day-to-day conversation, the artificial languages of the sciences and the language of art. Lotman is clear about the difference between the language outside literature and the language of literature. Stating how language functions in the domain of art (read literature), he writes:

> First it permits us to single out those characteristics which art holds in common with every language, and attempt to describe those characteristics in the general form of a theory of signs. Second, it permits us, in light of the first description, to single out that which is inherent to art as a special language and which distinguishes art from other systems of this type. (8)

Lotman rightly states that the language of the artistic text has something in common with ordinary language but it also possesses some exclusive features which make it a special language. We are all conversant with the idea that ordinary language, like Coleridge's primary imagination, is the base on which the special language of literature builds up a beautiful edifice. Words like 'unique', 'special' and 'exclusive' recur in Lotman's writings in the context of literature, which is a fitting reply to Derrida's sweeping generalizations about the nature of language and literature, although Lotman does not seem familiar with Derrida's writings published around the same time as his. Using the same Saussurean linguistics that Derrida draws on, Lotman arrives at the following conclusion:

> Literature speaks in *special language* which is superimposed as a secondary system on natural language. (21, emphasis added)

> To say that literature has its own language ... is merely another way of saying that literature possesses an *exclusive*, inherent system of signs and rules .... (21, emphasis added)

> ... each artistic text is created as a *unique* sign with a particular content, constructed ad hoc. (22, emphasis added)

The italicized words in these citations mark literature off from other kinds of writings. That the language of literature is unique, special, and exclusive sufficiently counters Derrida's strident denial of any special status to literature and its language.

In order to establish a unique identity of literature, Lotman goes beyond language to artistic creation. Lotman says time and again that the language of an artistic text creates a model of the universe. An artist does not give us mere ideas or information as we find them in non-literature. An idea for him is an image, which is a verbal equivalent of a physical entity in the world. I am giving below three extracts from Lotman containing this concept:

> An idea in art is always a model, for it reconstructs an image of reality. (12)

> The language of an artistic text is, in essence, an artistic model of the universe .... (18)

> Signs in art are iconic and representational rather than conventional as in language .... A sign models its content. (21)

It is the third citation which contains the clue to Lotman's central idea in these extracts. That signs in literature are icons is an idea with which students of Anglo-American criticism are well familiar. The idea first introduced by Charles S. Peirce has been used by several critics, including J.C. Ransom who sets great store by image which lends concrete form to abstract ideas to which worldly objects are reduced. Although he does not say it in so many words, Lotman seems to go beyond these critics in maintaining that the writer creates a model of the universe. The writer builds up his own universe with the use of images; he creates another universe inhabited not only by what we come across in the world but also what are imaginary creatures such as unicorns, centaurs and dragons as well as gods, goddess, ghosts and witches. They are all in the literary universe not as abstract ideas but in flesh and blood. It is in Shakespear's tragedies that we see what ghosts and witches look like and how they behave. Do we find such creations in other disciplines with which Derrida identifies literature?

Another idea expressed by Lotman in the above citation as well as elsewhere is the inseparability of idea from the total literary construct in which it is concretized. Hence, his rejection of any separable content or message. He uses an analogy to express this idea. The house is built according to a plan which is the architect's idea, but the plan is realized in the total structure of the house, not in any of its components. Similarly 'an artistic idea is inconceivable outside a structure'(12). This comes strikingly close to Cleanth Brooks' view of 'the structure of poetry' and 'the heresy of paraphrase.' Whether expressed by Brooks or Lotman, the emphasis on image as well as the difference between image and idea is at odds with Derrida's deconstructive notion of the text which rejects any distinction between idea and image (read metaphor) and thereby establishes that languages as such is literature. Ironically enough, when Derrida undertakes a deconstructive reading of a text, say Saussure's *Course in General Linguistics,* he focuses on the idea rather than the image.

Lotman speaks of 'semantic saturation' in a literary text. He is of the opinion that the rich, multilayered meaning in a literary text cannot be communicated in ordinary language. 'A complicated artistic structure,' he writes 'created from the material of language, allows us to transmit a volume of information too great to be transmitted by an elementary, strictly linguistic, structure' (10). The multilayered 'semantic saturation' which has been termed 'ambiguity' by the British critic, William Empson, is not the same thing as Derrida's deconstructive dissemination which denies any logic or centre in any text. Both Empson and Lotman have faith in truth, logic and sense. In fact, Empson rejects his mentor, I.A. Richards's view that logic is absent from poetry and underlines the presence of sense in it. And Lotman unequivocally asserts that 'art is inseparable from the search for truth'(15).

Lotman has been discussed at some length in order to highlight the idea that the use of Saussure's linguistics does not necessarily mean the end of the identity of literature. Like Jakobson before him, Lotman has made an extensive use of Saussure's linguistics, but nowhere does he doubt that literature has an identity of its own, which is reflected in its special use of language.

In important ways Lotman anticipates Culler's poetics. Even the title of Culler's magnum opus, *Structuralist Poetics* (1975) is strikingly similar to Lotman's first work, *Lectures on*

Structural Poetics (1964). I am giving below some extracts from Lotman's *The Structure of the Artistic Text,* which foreshadow Culler's critical postulates:

> Art is a secondary modelling system ... secondary modelling systems, like all semiotic systems, are constructed on the model of language. (9)

> It we take a large group of functionally similar texts and view them as variants on one invariant text removing everything that is extrasystemic from our point of view, we arrive at a structural description of the language of the group of texts. (15)

> Since it can concentrate a tremendous amount of information into the 'area' of a very small text ... an artistic text manifests yes another feature: it transmits different information to different readers in proportion to each one's comprehension [read competence] .... (23)

The first statement by Lotman anticipates Culler's critical idea that linguistics can be looked upon as a model for poetics. To him, linguistics is to language as poetics is to literature. The similarity between Lotman's and Culler's views is evident from the following pronouncement of Culler:

> The proper and fruitful relationship between linguistics and literary criticism is one of analogy, or more precisely, of homology. That is to say, linguistics as a model for analysing a linguistic system provides a model which suggests how one might construct a poetics which would study literature as a system. (Culler, 1977: 93)

Both Lotman and Culler build up a poetics on the premises supplied by Saussure's structural linguistics. They are clear about the distinction between linguistics and poetics: one deals with language while the other with literature. The second excerpt from Lotman cited makes use of Saussure's distinction between *langue* and *parole* which finds its echo in Culler's formulation of the poetics of the lyric and the novel, while the third extract points to Culler's reader-responsism. In the chapters on the lyric and the novel, Culler evolves what Lotman calls the 'invariant text' which manifets itself in different manifestations of the two literary forms. His reader-responism studies how different meanings are discovered in the same text by different readers.

Behind both Lotman and Culler looms the gigantic figure of Roman Jakobson. But there is a difference between Jakobson and Lotman, on the one hand and Culler on the other. While the former are known for their objectivity which springs from their dependence on Saussure, the latter, though drawing on the same source, shares the subjectivity of reader-response critics with whom he is grouped.

Culler seeks to establish not that literature does not exist but that literariness is generated by the reader with the use of the system or grammar of literature which he has assimilated. In the absence of the system stored in his mind, he will be unable to recognize a piece of literature as literature, let alone appreciate it. The same piece of writing can be ordinary or literary depending on the reading strategy that the reader employs, argues Culler. The following quotations from his *Structuralist Poetics* bring out his central argument:

> The semiological approach suggests rather that the poem be thought of as an utterance that has meaning only with respect to a system of conventions which the reader has assimilated. If other conventions were operative, its range of potential meanings would be different. (Culler, 1975: 116)

> But the fact that a text is a poem is not the necessary result of its linguistic properties, and attempts to base a theory of poetry on an account of the special properties of the language of poems seem doomed to failure. (Culler, 1975: 162)

Between these two citations, Culler has suggested that the poem does not have an identity of its own, as it is created ad hoc by the reader with the use of a system of reading conventions. This is an extreme position taken by Culler. What is the source of the 'system of conventions' which the reader assimilates and employs in responding to poetry? Does he derive it from the experience of reading journalistic writings or any writing for that matter written in what we take as ordinary language or is it the corollary of his experience of reading poetry? If it is the latter which is the likely answer, then what Culler is saying has always been maintained by literary critics from Aristotle onwards. The difference is only in the way of presenting the idea. Is it not said that Aristotle derived his critical ideas formulated in his *poetics* out of his experience of existing literature? The response to literature varies from reader to reader and hence we have different theories of literature and literary forms.

Culler seeks to convey that, as there are no special properties of the language of poetry, a text in ordinary prose can be transformed into a literary text and vice verse by simply changing the strategies of reading conventions. He himself converted a prose line from Quine into a poem by changing its form to verse, which implies that the opposite is also possible. Let us take the example cited by Culler himself. Culler examines Pound's celebrated two-line poem, 'In a Station of the Metro':

The apparition of these faces in the crowd;
Petals on a wet, black bough.

Culler comments that the poem 'asks to be taken as a perception of 'inscape', a moment of revelation in which form is grasped and surface becomes profundity' (1975: 175). This is tantamount to saying that the poem directs the reader as to how it has to be responded to. This is not possible unless there is something in the language and the structure of the poem which gives the reader the impression that it is a poem, and a poem of some worth, which calls for serious attention. Culler's argument that any text in ordinary language can be converted into a piece of literature by simply changing the 'system of conventions' does not carry conviction. The opening sentence of Quine's 'From a Logical Point of view': 'The curious thing about the ontological problem is its simplicity,' does not invite, even in its changed form, the kind of attention that Pound's poem deserves and receives. The absence of what Lotman calls 'semantic saturation' is felt by the reader.

It is interesting to note that the system of the lyric that Culler evolves is predicated on the New Critical concepts which are time and again invoked by him. William Empson whose *Seven Types of Ambiguity* was the first important critical work by a new critic, figures prominently in Culler's discussion of the lyric. Culler assumes that Empson's ambiguity and Brooks's paradox are part of the system of the lyric which the reader naturalizes and exploits in his response to the lyric. Distance and impersonality, organic unity, epiphanic revelation of the meaning and metaphor which go into the making of Culler's poetics of the lyric are familiar critical ideas which we associate with the New Critics. In fact, Culler is in large measure in consonance with the New Critics. Where he differs with them is in denying that the properties of poetry stated by them inhere in the text. To him, they are simply discerned by the competent reader with the help of the strategies of reading conventions. The difference between Culler and the New Critics is only in the way of presenting their ideas.

Culler falls in line with critics like Jakobson and Lotman who draw on Saussure's linguistics to build up a theory which distinguishes literature from non-literature. It hardly matters, if for Culler it is the reader who creates the distinct identity of literature, not any exclusive literary properties.

As is obvious from the foregoing discussions, literature exists with its distinct identity notwithstanding Derrida and his acolytes' arguments to the contrary. Derrida's levelling of the distinction between literature and other disciplines is at best a purely academic exercise which has had little impact on the common reader's response to literature, who continues to enjoy and appreciate literature as distinct from non-literature.

Works Cited

Culler, Jonathan. *Structuralist Poetics.* Ithaca, N.Y.: Cornell University Press, 1975.

——. 'Linguistics as a Model for Poetics'. *Twentieth Century American Criticism: Interdisciplinary Approaches,* ed. Rajnath. New Delhi: Arnold Heinemann, 1977.

Eichenbaum, Boris. 'The Theory of the Format Method.' *Russian Formalist Criticism,* ed. L.T. Lemon and Marion J. Reis. Lincoln, Nebr. University of Nebraska Press, 1965.

Jakobson, Roman. 'Linguistics and Poetics?' In *Style in Language,* ed. Thomas A. Sebeok. Cambridge, Mass. M.I.T, 1960.

Lotman, Jürij. *The Structure of the Artistic Text,* tr. Gail Lenhoff and Ronald Vroon. Michigan: The University of Michigan Press, 1977.

Saussure, Ferdinand de. *Course in General Linguistics,* tr. Wade Baskin. New York: McGraw-Hill Book Company, 1966.

CHAPTER 5

Fictionality and the Identity of Literature

The present chapter replies to Derrida's questioning of a distinct identity of literature by focusing on one of its exclusive features, i.e. fictionality.

That the domain of literature is fictional has been generally admitted by philosophers and literary theorists down the centuries. Plato and Aristotle in the classical Age, Sidney during the Renaissance, Samuel Johnson in the new-classical age and several critics and philosophers of language in the twentieth century have debated the nature and function of the fictional world.

John Crowe Ransom lists fictionality, along with metre and trope, as the devices that poets employ to express their perceptual impulse which he contrasts with the practical impulse of scientists. Throughout his brief discussion of fictionality, Ransom contrasts the fictional and the actual, the former being the territory of poetry and the latter of science.

Of poetry he writes: 'Over every poem which looks like a poem is a sign which reads: This road does not go through the action; fictitious.'(131) Ransom argues that the object described by art does not have an actual existence and as such gives only an 'illusion of reality'. He lends credence to Kant's view that the authentic judgement is 'so far from depending on the object's existence that it really depends on the object's non-existence.'(Qtd. in Ransom, 131) Ransom's assertion that the objects in the world of art are mere Illusion of objects is no disparagement of art, although he goes some distance with Plato as in the following citation:

> If jealous science succeeds in keeping the field of history for its own exclusive use, it does not therefore annihilate the arts, for they reappear in a field which may be called real *though one degree removed from actuality.* (132) (emphasis added)

The italicized portion may give the impression that the world of art is inferior to the world we inhabit, but this is not Ransom's intention. Unlike Plato, Ransom believes that the fictional world of art is superior to the surrounding world. He takes a hypothetical case. Suppose we enjoy an object in the world of art and subsequently find the same object in the real world. Which one shall we prefer? Presumably the former, as we do not enjoy the real object as much as its artistic representation. Moreover, there are other considerations in the real world such as the desire to possess the object and we may not have the wherewithal to buy it. All this goes to prove that to Ransom, fictional representation is not only different from but superior to the real world.

In an essay published as late as 2009, Maximilian De Gaynesford takes up once again the issue relating to the fictional and imaginative character of poetry and the seriousness and otherwise of poetic statements. He has taken stock of the controversy between the philosophers of language, J.L. Austin and John Searle, on the one hand, and poet Geoffrey Hill and scholar Christopher Ricks on the other. Gaynesford finds the crux of the matter enshrined in the following statement by Austin:

> And I might mention that, quite differently again, we could be issuing any of these utterances as we can issue an utterance of any kind whatsoever, in the course, for example, of acting a play or making a joke or writing a poem in which case of course it would not be seriously meant and we shall not be able to say that we seriously performed the act concerned. (Qtd. in Gaynesford, 1)

The controversy that stems from this pronouncement centres on Austin's attitude towards drama and poetry which Hill and Ricks find dismissive. At any rate, Austin's clubbing of poetry and the utterance by an actor in a dramatic performance with joking is unfortunate, as joking is not a serious utterance, but what an actor speaks on the stage or a poet says in his poem, is sincerely and seriously communicated to and taken by the audience. Austin's argument is that all the three are identical speech acts, as in all of them saying does not result in deed. The point is well taken but the parallel ends here. A joke is cracked and received in the real world in a particular situation and the communication takes place between persons who know each other. But when an actor on the stage or a poet in his poem speaks even to the audience who know them, they presume that the speaker is making an imaginative enactment and he is different from the person they know. Hence a joke may not be taken seriously but the speech by an actor or a passage in a poem is taken in a different spirit which is far from non-serious.

Gaynesford's quotation from Austin comes from the latter's essay on 'Performative Utterances' included in his *Philosophical Papers* where joke is perched oddly between drama and poetry. But Austin seems aware of the difference, which has escaped the attention of Geynesford, between a joke and the utterance by an actor in a dramatic performance and a character in a poem and hence he refrains from taking the example of joking and replaces it with soliloquy in *How to do Things with Words,* where he writes:

> ... a performative utterance will, for example, be in a peculiar way hollow or void, if said by an actor on the stage or introduced in a poem or spoken in a soliloquy ... . Language in such circumstances is in special ways—intelligibly — used not seriously, but in a way *parasitic* upon its normal use—ways which *fall* under the doctrine of the *etiolations of language.* (22)

Austin believes the trio mentioned by him make statements, or perform, to use Austin's term, speech acts which cannot be taken seriously, as they do not result in deeds. 'Go and catch a falling star' in Donne's poem, for example, is not an order in the usual sense to perform a deed. The two words in the above citation, 'parasitic' and 'etiolations' have obvious pejorative implications which undermine the status of literary creativity.

Geoffrey Hill and Christopher Ricks take umbrage at Austin's 'not seriously' in the statement above as if Austin's denigration of poetry were like Plato's and therefore they felt it incumbent upon them to defend it as Aristotle did in the ancient past. The controversy took on the complexion of philosophy versus poetry as is evident from Hill's rebuttal. 'It is a 'philosophical irony', says Hill, that a mind which strove for accuracy of definition, felt free to regard poetry as one of the non-serious 'parasitic', 'etiolations of language', as a kind of joking.' (Qtd.in Gaynesford, 3) As a poet he cannot accept that poetry is what Austin makes of it. He turns the tables on Austin in his poem 'On the Reality of the Symbol', where he calls metaphysics a joke: 'Metaphysics remain/In common language something of a joke.' Hill's reply is tit for tat. The philosopher and the poet are at daggers drawn. Austin 'unprincipled levity' is answered with levity.

Ricks is less vitriolic in his critique of Austin's view of poetry. He agrees with Austin that 'performative-apt utterances in poetry do not perform' but he cannot accept that poetry is non-serious. He appreciates Austin's sensibility and his sensitivity to words as they function in and outside literature and, therefore, his aversion to and dismissal of poetry can be accounted for only in terms of professional rivalry, 'a philosopher's slighting of the poet's enterprise'. (ibid. 6)

John Searle defends Austin by saying that he is concerned with the way words function in speech acts and hence he rightly excludes from consideration non-standard speech acts like utterances by actors on the stage or novelists in their novels:

> Austin's idea is simply this: if we want to know what it is to make a promise or to make a statement, we had better not start our investigation with promise by actors on a stage in the course of a play or statements made in a novel by novelists about characters in the novel because in a fairly obvious way such statements are not standard cases of promise and statements .... (Qtd. in Culler, 117)

Searle also leaves out joking and restricts himself to literary creativity in major literary forms like drama and the novel, though one fails to understand why he leaves out poetry. Although Searle replaces Austin's 'non-serious' with his 'non-standard', there is hardly any difference in the attitude towards imaginative literature. Both are dismissive of literature if literary utterances are only fictional and as such do not result in deeds.

Austin's argument that words in poetry, or in any form of literature for that matter, do not result in deeds is unexceptionable. It is, perhaps, this gap between words and deed in the domain of poetry which makes Auden blurt out in his elegy on W.B. Yeats that 'poetry makes nothing happen'. That words are not deeds in the imaginative world of literature has never been questioned, though these words can propel people to deeds in the real world. It seems that what has offended Hill so much is the joking with which poetry is clubbed by Austin and which has rightly been dropped by him elsewhere. Ricks's reaction is more sobre and sensitive. As Ransom has argued, fictionality is one of the essential features of poetry. There is a striking similarity between Ransom and Austin as far as fiction in poetry is concerned, but they differ in their assessment. If Austin had not aimed at a disparagement of poetry by calling it non-serious, he would have helped us in our endeavour to identify literature. In fact, the weakness that Austin discovers in literature is the very factor that seperates it from non-literature and thereby lends is a distinct identity.

If Hill and Ricks attack Austin for what they consider the philosopher's dismissal of literature, Derrida at the other end of the spectrum cuts the ground from under his feet by converting philosophy itself into literature. Fictionality is no longer confined to literature but is inexorably present in all writings including philosophy. The very distinction between the real and the imaginative, the factual and the fictional is demolished. As is well known, Derrida does not accept the two-language theory propounded by philosophers and literary theorists and instead forcefully pleads for only one language which is literary.

Austin's distinction between constantive and performative utterances, the former which answer the question of true or false and the latter which does not, and his argument that the performative is dependent on the constantive has been subjected to a deconstructive analysis by Derrida in his 'Signature, Even, Context', where he concludes that 'these effects [of the constantive] do not exclude what is generally opposed to them term by term, but, on the contrary' presupposed it in the dissymmetrical fashion the general space of their possibility' (1982: 327). Derrida believes that the distinction between serious and non-serious utterances is untenable. If serious utterance tells or intends to tell the truth, then for Derrida there is no such utterance, as all utterances are in the nature of literary utterance which has nothing to do with truth. If the meaning of an utterance is determined by the context, then no determinate meaning will inhere in Austin's serious utterance, as the same sentence can be uttered in an endless number of contexts generating disparate meanings. Turning the tables on Austin, Derrida writes: 'no meaning can be determined out of context, but no context permits saturation.' (1979: 81) The one distinction which is often drawn between imaginative and non-imaginative, or fictional and factual writings, is that in the former meaning is indeterminate while in the latter it is determinate. But meaning, argues Derrida, is always indeterminate and 'illimitable', as the context which determines meaning is itself unlimited. What Derrida misses in Austin's philosophy of language is that the constantive is the fixed meaning of a sentence, while the performative is its variable meaning depending on the context. Austin is right in saying that the constantive is the base on which the performative depends. It is after a lot of hair-splitting' that Derrida completes his deconstructive demolition of Austin hierarchies of constantive/performative and serious/non-serious.

Both Hill and Derrida oppose Austin, but their responses are radically different. Hill objects to Austin's calling literature non-serious, a kind of joking and dismisses philosophy itself as a kind of joking. However, he is at one with Austin in viewing philosophy and literature as independent entities. Derrida ends once and for all the conflict between philosophers and literatuers by dissolving the very distinction between their respective disciplines. If literature is non-serious, philosophy is just as non-serious, if serious means truthful and factual. Discussing the identity of philosophy as well as literature in the wake of Deconstruction, Alan Bass writes:

> What then does one call the writing, the text in which philosophical concepts turn against themselves, explode themselves, in order to demonstrate their own (im)possibility, their irreducible doubleness. Since they obey no philosophical regulations of truth, these texts have a certain 'fictive' or 'literary' quality .... (349)

Alan Bass seeks to explain the status of literature as well as philosophy in deconstruction. Literature no longer enjoys the privileged place that it once did, as philosophical text (and by implication all texts reckoned non-literary) do not, and cannot, follow the 'philosophical regulations' of truth, since they have the fictionality of literary constructs. Thus, the new concept of literature eliminates the distinction between imaginative and factual writings, as all writings take on literary complexion.

Derrida's deconstructive speculations which level all distinctions of genres and concepts have not gone unchallenged. Umberto Eco, an eminent semiotician, a fine novelist, and a perceptive literary critic, reinforces the distinction between the imaginative and factual writings in his book, *On Literature.* In one place in the book, he comments upon the difference between the real world in which we live, act and communicate and the fictional world created by writers. The passage is too important to be curtailed and, therefore, it is being cited in full:

> On one hand the world seems to be a 'closed' book, allowing of only one reading. If, for example, there is a law governing planetary gravitation, then it is either the right one or the wrong one. Compared with that, the universe of a book seems to us to be an open universe. But let us try to approach a narrative work with common sense and compare the assumptions we make about it with those we can make about the world. As far as the world is concerned, we find that the laws of universal gravitation are those established by Newton, or that it is true that Napoleon died on Saint Helena on 5 May 1821. And yet, if we keep an open mind, we will always be prepared to revise our convictions the day science formulates the great laws of the cosmos differently, or a historian discovers unpublished documents proving that Nepoleon died on a Bonapartist

> ship as he attempted to esape. On the other hand, as far as the world of books is concerned, propositions like 'Sherlock Holmes was a bachelor,' 'Little Red Riding-Hood is eaten by the wolf and then freed by the woodcutter,' or 'Anna Karenina commits suicide' will remain true for eternity, and no one will ever be able to refute them. There are people who deny that Jesus was the son of God, others who doubt his historical existence, others who claim he is the Way, the Truth, and the Life, and still others who believe that the Messiah is yet to come, and *hower* we might think about such questions, we treat these opinions with respect. But there is little respect for those who claim that Hamlet married Ophelia, or that Superman is not Clerk Kent. (15)

Eco's distinction between the world and the book is tantamount to the difference between the factual and the fictional writings. His observation goes contrary to the common belief that the real world is authentic, whereas the fictional world is subject to change. For Eco, it is the other way round. In the real world, which is rooted in facts, it is possible to question and alter a fact but such a questioning or alteration is not possible in the imaginative world created by the artist, as whatever is in the world of literature is irrevocably present there for all times.

In a vein similar to that of Eco, Herbert Marcuse believes that the represented reality of art, although fictitious, is more real and truthful than the external reality:

> ... The World of a work of art is 'unreal' in the ordinary sense of the word; it is a fictitious reality. But it is 'unreal' not because it is less, but because it is more as well as qualitatively 'other' than the established reality. As fictitious world, as illusion (Schein), it contains more truth than does everyday reality .... (54)

Marcuse reverses the polarities while accepting the basic assumption of Austin and Searle that literary world is fictional. To him, fictionality makes reality more real and truthful. However, Marcuse is also aware of the limitation of art, as is evidenced by his utterance, which resonates Austin's view, that 'art cannot translate its vision into reality' as it remains a 'fictitious' world (57). But this limitation, argues Marcuse, does not detract from art, which transforms transitory historical reality into something richer and more enduring.

Jonathan Culler, who has built his poetics on the model of linguistics, discerns the fictionality of literature in its language. He takes as his example the use of deictics and anaphorics which do not function in literature in any of the ways they function outside literature. The 'deictic' is explained by *Oxford Advanced Learner's Dictionary,* 8th Edition (2010), as 'relating to a word or expression whose meaning depends on who says it, where they are, who they are talking to, etc, for example 'you', 'me', 'here', 'next week'.' In ordinary discourse, it is easy to answer these questions, but in literary discourse we can answer them only through an imaginative construction. Cullar takes the example of Shelley's 'The Cloud' whose 'I', the speaker in the poem, is the cloud, but that is acceptable only in the fictional world of literature.

What is true of deictic also holds for the anaphoric article 'the'. Culler here takes the example of W.B. Yeats' 'Leda and the Swan', where the article 'the' does not function in any of the following ways in which it does in ordinary discourse:

1. to isolate a general class
2. to indicate a concern with a particular member/item of the class.

3. to refer to something/someone already mentioned

In the line '*The* Great Wings beating still/Above *the* staggering girl' (Culler's emphasis), 'the' is not functioning in any of the ways stated above. On the use of the definite article in the poem, Culler Writes:

> It is not the staggering girl as opposed to some other girl, nor is it the great wings as opposed to some small ones. The definite articles are not working in this way, nor of course, are they isolating a general class ('the staggering girl is a peculiar species'), they are working anaphorically, referring us back to a previous mention. But, of course, there is no previous mention except in the title, so it is as if the poem were forcing us to refer to a scene or a situation we must imagine. (Culler, 1977, 95)

Culler's observations suggest that when we read a work of literature, we enter a world of fiction in which the reader keeps reconstructing scenes and situations with the help of his imagination in order to make sense of the text.

Besides the question of veracity, the fictional world created by imagination has a quality which is altogether absent from the real world. The literary world renders pleasure and pleasure only, whereas the real world gives sometimes pleasure and sometimes pain. Even painful experiences of life become a source of aesthetic pleasure. Commenting on art experience according to Indian aesthetics, M. Hiriyanna writes that ' it yields a kind of joy which is pure and unstained by the least pain' (164). This is similar to Wordsworth's view expressed in the 'Preface' that in the aesthetic universe created by the poet 'whenever we sympathize with pain it will be found that the sympathy is produced and carried on with subtle combinations of pleasure.' (173)

We must not forget that the aesthetic pleasure that we experience in the domain of literature is different from the ordinary pleasure in the real world. Aesthetic pleasure comes out of verbal representations of external objects which are absent as external stimuli. The writer creates with his artistic skills another world, which is more real than the real world in which the reader experiences pure joy.

The fictionality described above is an important point of difference between literature and non-literature. A reader-response critic like Jonathan Culler will say that the fictionality is created by the reader with the help of reading conventions. But this is only partly true. It is primarily the product of the writer's imagination and the reader makes his own contribution while experiencing it.

Works Cited

Austin, J.L. *How to Do Things with Words.* Cambridge, Mass.: Harvard University Press, 1975.

Bass, Alan. "'Literature'/Literature". *Velocities of Change,* ed. Richard Mackey. Baltimore: The Johns Hopkins University Press, 1974.

Culler, Jonathan. *On Deconstruction.* London: Routledge and Kegan Paul, 1983.

——. 'Linguistics as a Model for Poetics.' *Twentieth Century American Criticism: Interdisciplinary Approaches* ed. Rajnath. New Delhi: Arnold- Heinemann, 1977.

Derrida, Jacques. 'Living on: Borderlines'. *Deconstruction and Criticism,* ed. Harold Bloom, etc. New York: Continuum, 1979.

——. *Margins of Philosophy*, trans. Alan Bass. Sussex: Harvester University Press, 1982.

Eco, Umberto. *On Literature* trans. Martin McLaughtin. London: Vintage, 2006.

Gaynesford, Maximilian De. 'The Seriousness of Poetry,' *Essays in Criticism*, Vol. LIX (January), 2009.

Hiriyanna, M. 'Some Aspects of Indian Aesthetics.' *Indian Aesthetics*, ed. V.S. Seturaman. Calcutta: Macmillan India, 1964.

Marcuse, Herbert. *The Aesthetic Dimension*. Boston: Beacon Press, 1978.

Ransom J.C. *The World's Body*. Baton Rouge: Louisiana State University Press, 1968.

Wordsworth, William. 'Preface to *Lyrical Ballads*.' *English Critical Texts*, ed. D.J. Enright and Ernst de Chickera. Delhi: Oxford University Press, 1975.

Chapter 6

Literature and Experience

In his *Poetry and Experience,* Archibald MacLeish refers to the Chinese poet, Lu Chi's prose poem on literature whose central idea is that 'the begetting of a poem involves not a single electric pole thrust deep into the acids of the self but a pair of poles—a man and the world opposite.' (15) This is true of all kinds and forms of literature, not only poetry. But we must bear in mind that experience is not synonymous with emotion or feeling but a blend of emotion and thought, or feeling and understanding. The writer not only feels the world but also thinks about it.

Rasa is the fulcrum of Sanskrit poetics. Although it is difficult to find its exact equivalent in English, it can be translated as 'aesthetic mood', or 'aesthetic experience', or simply as 'emotion', but this is what is experienced by the reader in the course of his enjoyment of literature and not the emotion of the writer. It is interesting that Eliot has used the term 'art emotion' while delineating different kinds of emotion in his celebrated essay on tradition:

> It is not in his *personal emotion* evoked by particular events in his life, that the poet is in any way remarkable or great. (20, emphasis added).

> This is so to speak the *structural emotion* [the balance of the contrasted emotions of beauty and ugliness in an extract cited] provided by the drama. But the whole effect, the dominant tone, is due to the fact that a number of *floating feelings,* having an affinity to this emotion by no means superficially evident, have combined with it to give us new *art emotion.* (57, emphasis added)

Here Eliot comes strikingly close to Sanskrit critics to whom what matters is the depersonalized emotion combodied in a work of art. Eliot is known for his impersonal theory of poetry and Sanskrit theorists have formulated the concept of *sadharanikaran* (generalization) of emotion in a work of art. Eliot has distinguished between three kinds of emotion in the above extracts but Sanskrit poetics divide it into eight or nine different kinds with *shringar (erotic emotion)* taking the pride of place.

It is said that in Western criticism, the focus is on the writer whereas Sanskrit poetics is centred on the reader, the reader being a *sahriday* (a sensitive reader). But the fact of the matter is that the reader in Western criticism, though not always foregrounded, is always implied, as critics like Plato, Aristotle, Longinus, Horace, Sidney, Johnson, Wordsworth, Coleridge, Arnold as well as I.A. Richards and T.S. Eliot have the reader in mind while formulating their critical concepts. Of course, the reader is taken for granted and not subjected to scrutiny as in reader-response criticism in the West, which emerged late in the twentieth century or Sanskrit poetics in India going back to Bharat of the 2nd century B.C. Whether the focus is on the writer or the reader, the problems relating to the identity of literature are more or less the same.

In both Western and Oriental criticism, literature is contrasted with what is non-literature which is designated by the term *sastra* in Sanskrit poetics and science in Western criticism meaning by science not only disciplines of pure sciences but also those in humanities and social sciences which aim at scientific objectivity.

The watertight division between literature and other disciplines made in both Western and Oriental criticism is untenable, but at the same time the extreme position of Derrida and his followers, which dissolves all distinctions between them is not acceptable either. In fact, science is not without imagination and literature is not altogether devoid of logic. A certain element of subjectivity, imagination and literariness does inform science, law, philosophy, history, psychology, etc. and similarly the element of logic premised on the denotative property of language does find a place in literature. The emotion-reason dichotomy postulated by the critics of the past is not borne out by the actual practice of literary and non-literary writings. Approaching literature from the standpoint of *rasa* theory, V.K. Chari writes:

> *rasa* theory asserts not simply that poetry expresses emotions but that the expression of emotions is the sole aim and the common denominator of all literary productions. (9)

Sanskrit poetics is basically romantic criticism where an exclusive emphasis is laid on subjectivity and emotion. In Sanskrit poetics, there is a gap between the concept of language and the concept of literature. Denotative property of language is never denied in Sanskrit poetics and it is the denotation which is the vehicle of reason, logic and truth. What emerge from Sanskrit poetics is that denotation is the foundation on which the edifice of *lakshna (*indication)and *vyanjana* (implication or suggestion) is built. If this is so, then literature cannot be viewed as communicating emotion only. Coleridge is right when he distinguishes between science and poetry by saying that the immediate object of the former is truth, while the immediate object of the latter is pleasure. 'A poem,' writes Coleridge, 'is that species of composition, which is opposed to works of science, by proposing for its *immediate* object pleasure, not truth' (10) Pleasure in the former and truth in the latter can have and does have a secondary place. When science attains its goal, pleasure and that of the highest kind results, says Coleridge, but it is not its immediate end and similarly truth or logic is not altogether absent from poetry, though it occupies a secondary place. The list of opposites which are brought to reconciliation by Coleridge's secondary or literary imagination includes the binaries of idea and image, order and emotion, and judgement and enthusiasm. Coleridge knows that even though pleasure, emotion, or sentiment is the immediate object of literature, it needs to be held in check by order and judgement exercised by logic and reason.

M.H. Abrams is his classic *The Mirror and the Lamp* makes a watertight division of criticism into romantic and classical. He believes that in romantic criticism, the poet's mind is viewed as a lamp which radiates light on external reality whereas in classical and neoclassical criticism, the poet's mind is compared to a mirror which imitates external reality.[1] M.H. Abrams's scholarship is beyond doubt and his book teems with brilliant critical insights. But when he examines English romantic criticism in his introductory chapter, he focuses on critics like Shelley, Keats and Mill whose opinions support his thesis and leaves out such a perceptive critic like Coleridge presumably because his opinion goes contrary to Abrams's basic premises. When he cites Wordsworth's definition of poetry, he reproduces only the first part of the definition, where Wordsworth defines poetry as 'the spontaneous overflow of powerful feelings' and leaves out the second part where he says that 'it is emotion recollected in tranquillity.' Recollection is done through a thinking process, and the recollected emotion is not as spontaneous as the original emotion. Moreover, words like truth and knowledge occur frequently is Wordsworth's 'Preface' where he discusses the nature and function of poetry:

> Poems to which any value can be attached were never produced on any variety of subjects but by a man who, being possessed more than usual organic sensibility, had also thought long and deeply. (Enright and Chickera, 165, emphasis added.)

> Aristotle, I have been told, has said that poetry is the most philosophical of all writing: it is so: its object is *truth*, not individual and local but general, and operative, not standing upon external reality, but carried alive into the heart by passion. (ibid., 173, emphasis added)

> The Poet, singing a song in which all human beings join with him, rejoices in the presence of *truth* as our visible friend and hourly companion. Poetry is the breath and finer spirit of all knowledge .... (Ibid., 174, emphasis added)

> The poet binds together by passion and *knowledge.* The vast empire of human society. (ibid., 175, emphasis added)

> Poetry is the first and last of all knowledge ... . (ibid., emphasis added)

The above extracts from Wordsworth's "Preface' to *Lyrical Ballads'* leave us in no doubt that to Wordworth poetry is not out and out subjective or emotional. Poetry to him combines passion and pleasure with truth and knowledge.

Coleridge and Wordsworth are the two pillars of English romantic criticism. The upshot of their views is that science aims at truth which it arrives at by using logic but poetry, and by extension literature in general, blends emotions and feelings with logic and truth. By postulating the presence of truth and knowledge (Wordsworth) as well as ideas, order and judgement (Coleridge) in literature they run contrary to Derrida who believes that literature, or the language of literature, for that matter, does not and cannot, express truth.

Of the modern critics, T.S. Eliot was the first to question the romantic concept of poetry, especially the one formulated by Wordsworth. In his essay on 'Tradition and the Individual Talent', he rejects out of hand Wordsworth's definition of poetry:

> We must believe that 'emotion recollected in tranquility' is an inexact formula. For it is neither emotion, nor recollection, nor without distortion of meaning, tranquillity. (21)

Eliot's rejection of the romantic emphasis on emotion may give one the impression that he veers round to the other extreme of thought and ratiocination in poetry. But, in fact, Eliot's criticism is best seen as combining the strands of romanticism and neo-classicism, which results in his blend of emotion and thought in poetry. This is borne out by his theory of the 'unification of sensibility' which is premised on the union of thought and emotion or what he calls 'emotional equivalent of thought', which he finds in the English metaphysical poets of whom he writes:

> It is to be observed that the language of these poets is as a rule simple and pure .... The structure of the sentences, on the other hand, is sometimes far from pure and simple, but this is not a vice; it is a fidelity to *thought and feeling.* (285, emphasis added)

The binary of thought and feeling unified by the poet's imagination is emphasized by Eliot throughout his writings. This marks him off from both the romantics and the neo-classicists. But there is another dimension of the thought-feeling combine: Eliot has something in common with both the romantics and the neo-classicists. This also dissipates the general impression that Eliot rejects emotion and feeling in favour of thought and intellect.

Eliot does attempt to correct the excesses of emotion in some romantic critics, particularly Shelley, but neither Wordsworth nor Coleridge leave out the element of thought in their theories of poetry. Eliot wants thought and feeling to go simultaneously, and not by turn as in the poetry of Tennyson and Browning. He never completely denies emotion, feeling or personality. If he stresses the ratiocinative, the intellectual element in poetry, it is only because he finds it lacking in the poetry written after the metaphysicals. In a significant utterance in his essay 'The Metaphysical Poets', Eliot says of Racine and Donne:

> Racine or Donne looked into a great deal more than the heart. One must look into the cerebral cortex, the nervous system, and the digestive tracts. (290)

That the poet has to look into 'a great deal more than the heart' does not imply that he does not have to look into the heart at all. Had this been so, Eliot would not have talked so often about emotions and feelings as necessary ingredients of poetry. Thought element is ineluctably present in literature alongiwth emotions and feelings.

Like Eliot, Leavis underscores the presence of thought in literary experience. His favourite terms, besides thought, are logic, intelligence and enquiring mind. In his three-part study of poetry published under the caption 'Judgement and Analysis', he examines in the first part, significantly titled 'Thought and Emotional Quality', the nature of literary experience and states unequivocally that in the absence of thought emotion is of poor quality.

Leavi's views experience critically and applauds poets and poems that do the same. The emotion in poetry has two dimensions, the emotion as such and the critical attitude towards emotion. The critical attitude is also the process of 'impersonalization' which is achieved with the use of 'critical mind'. In commenting upon Lawrence's 'Piano', Leavis makes a very perceptive observation.

> Something is, we see, held and presented in this poem, and the presenting involves an *attitude towards*, an element of disinterested valuation. For all the swell of emotion the critical mind has its part in the whole; constatation is at the same time in some measure a placing. That is, *sensibility in the poem does not work in complete divorce from intelligence; felling is not divorced from thinking*. (1968: 215–16; the second emphasis added)

It is abundantly clear from this citation that for Leavis, as for Eliot, emotion and thought can, and should, go together: separation of the two results in the banality of poetry.

Leavis is critical of those poems which are at the either extreme of emotion or thought. He takes up for comparison and evaluation a poem each by Wordsworth, Lawrence, Marvell, Tennyson, Shelley and Lionel Johnson. In the poems of the first three, Leavis discerns the blend of emotion and thought, emotion held in check and examined by thought, whereas in those of the last three, emotional sweep is uncotrolled in the absence of the questioning logic. A propos Johnson's poem 'By the Statue of king Charles at Charing Cross', he states that 'such impressiveness as Johnson's poem has is conditioned by an absence of thought.' (1968,222) He finds in the poem 'an absence of the questioning mind' and 'the essential absence of thought.' Leavis' emphasis on thought, logic and related terms keeps recurring throughout his critical writings. The main target of Leavis' attack is Shelley and of Shelley he says that the effect of his poetry 'depends on an abeyance of the demand for logic.' (1968: 225)

Leavis wants logic not merely in experience but also imagery which is the main technical device employed in poetry. He finds logic (at times the excess of it) in metaphysical imagery and a conspicuous absence of it in Shelley's imagery. It will be well to cite an extract from Leavis' chapter on Shelley in his *Revaluation* where he examines imagery in the second stanza of 'Ode to the West Wind' and finds it deficient in logic:

> In what respects are the 'loose clouds' like 'decaying leaves'? The correspondence is certainly not in shape, colour or way of moving. It is only the vague general sense of windy tumult that associates the clouds and the leaves and accordingly, the appropriateness of the metaphor 'stream' in the first line is not that it suggests a surface on which, like leaves, the clouds might be shed, but that it contributes to the general 'streaming' effect in which the inappropriateness of 'shed' passes unnoticed. (1964: 171)

Leavis' prime charge against Shelley's imagery is that it lacks logical appropriateness. Shelley, according to him, is a man of pure emotion, which is reflected in his poetry, in both its content and form.

Leavis' strident advocacy of logic in literature is a strong enough evidence to demolish Derrida's thesis that literary language is without logic and, since all manifestations of language are literary, there is no language which can communicate logic or truth. If literary language is not without logic, then certainly language outside literature cannot be said to be illogical.

Of the modern Western critics, Yvor Winters and J.C. Ransom have set maximum value on the logic in literature. Winters makes no bones about rationality in literature, as is evident from the title of his collected essays, *In Defence of Reason.* Even the subject that the writer seeks to express is rationally apprehended before it is emotionally felt. What gets finally expressed is the blend of thought and feeling:

> The poet ... understands his subject in rational terms and he so employs language that he communicates simultaneously that understanding and the feeling which it properly motivates. (503)

Poetry is, thus, the confluence of the rational and the emotional and not the one or the other exclusively.

Throughout his criticism, Winters argues that the poet expresses concept as well as the emotion which the concept evokes and, thus, differs from the scientist whose sole concern is with the concept. Comparing the scientist with the poet he writes:

> The scientist is interested in ideas, not in the feelings they motivate ... . The subject matter of poetry, on the other hand, is human experience. (506)

The binary of idea and experience, which are simultaneously present in literature, flies in the face of Derrida's deconstructive view of idea which is annihilated by its opposite and experience which is indistinguishable from idea. For Winters, the domain of science, and by extension of philosophy, consists of ideas whereas poetry communicates feeling alongwith ideas, as it is 'the concept which evokes the feeling'. (503) In fact, Winters is at the other extreme from Derrida. He finds logic strongly present in literature, whereas Derrida finds it absent from all disciplines, including literature. Demonstrating how a poem is composed, Winters writes:

> Now a poem is composed of words; that is, it is conceptual in its origin and it cannot escape from its origin. A poem about a tree is composed primarily of abstractions and secondarily of the feelings aroused by these abstractions: the tree, its leaves, its bark, its greenness, its brownness, its roughness, its smoothness, its strength, its motion, and all its other qualities, must be indicated in terms which are primarily conceptual. These terms, however, all suggest certain loose possibilities in the way of perception and feeling; and the poet's business is to relate them, or others similar to them, that a single and definite idea emerges, in company with a mental image of some aspect of a tree and in such a way that the feeling is communicated which is appropriate to the total idea-image both as a whole and with respect to each detail as one comes to it in reading. (503)

Winters is highlighting the role of the concept in a literary composition and how an object like tree described in literature combines idea with image. The idea-image combine tells us precisely what obtains in the domain of literature and how a work of literature renders the idea of a worldly object in concrete form. This is reminiscent of Coleridge's secondary imagination which reconciles idea with image.

In his aesthetics, John Crowe Ransom goes beyond Winters in his view that literature communicates knowledge of a particular kind, not emotions and feelings. He rejects the idea so often expressed by literary critics that literature and science are diametrically opposed to each other, the former imparting knowledge and the latter pleasure and sets forth his theory of literature as knowledge. He establishes a new relationship between science and literature, where they have the same objective, though they adopt different methods to achieve it.

Ransom agues that science communicates one kind of knowledge and literature another kind, but both the knowledges are equally valuable. Science provides the knowledge of the universals and literature the knowledge of the particulars and as such they complement each other. 'The scientific and aesthetic ways of knowledge,' writes Ransom, 'should illuminate each other; perhaps, they are alternative knowledges and a preference for one knowledge over the other might indicate an elemental or primary bias in temperament.' (1972: 13) Science and literature perform different tasks and therefore one cannot be judged by the standards of the other. Although Ransom believes that the two disciplines are not altogether exclusive, as literature is not without scientific logic and science is not completely devoid of artistic perception, the element of one discipline in the other is minimal. In his seminal essay, 'Poetry: A Note in Ontology', Ransom states:

> Science gratifies a rational or practical impulse and exhibits the minimum of perception. Art gratifies a perceptual impulse and exhibits the minimum of reason. (1965: 30)

Although Ransom discerns minimal reason or logic in literature, throughout his oeuvre he endeavours to defend logic in literature which is the source of a kind of knowledge that no other discipline can provide. Thus, Ransom's theory runs counter to Derrida's deconstruction which denies logic in literature and, since literature is made synonymous with language, in all verbal constructs.

According to Ransom, structure and texture which are respectively 'the logical meaning' and 'the local meaning' go into the making of a poem or any literary work, for that matter. He employs the image of a living room to drive home the relationship that obtains between the two:

> The walls of my room are obviously structural, the beams and the boards have a function, so does the plaster which is the visible aspect of the final wall. The plaster might have remained naked aspiring to no character and purely functional. But actually it has been painted receiving color, or it has been papered receiving color and design though these have no structural value and perhaps it has been hung with tapestry or with paintings for 'decoration'. The paint, the paper, the tapestry are texture. (1952: 233)

It is obvious from this citation that to Ransom, texture which is considered synonymous with literariness cannot exist without the prop of structure. One may not see the boards, the beams or the plaster but they do act as the foundation for the decoration on the walls with the paint, the paper, the tapestry, or paintings, which constitute texture and without which a work of art will lack aesthetic appeal.

Texture which is generated by imagery plays a significant role in Ransom's criticism. Ransom calls texture 'local' meaning, because it is texture which individualizes worldly phenomena and gives the kind of knowledge which to Ransom only literature can render. Ransom avers that 'imagination is an organ of knowledge whose technique is images,' (1968: 156) and that 'art exists for knowledge' (1972: 197). Contrasting the scientist's treatment of worldly objects with that of the artist, Ransom states that the former, by using universal signs, gives us 'a man' while the latter by using images provides us with 'this particular man' (1972: 6), with all the particularity that he possesses. This knowledge of the particulars can be provided only by literature as other disciplines can give us only the knowledge of the universals.

Though insufficiently recognized, Ransom has set forth a new aesthetics which centres on logic and knowledge by eliminating emotion from aesthetic experience. Ransom is not only challenging Western aesthetics going back to Plato and Aristotle but also Sanskrit poetics with its exclusive emphasis on emotive experience. Rejecting the focus on emotion in Western theories, Ransom writes:

> Poetry becomes slightly disreputable when regarded as not having any special or definable content, and as identified only by its capacity for teasing some dormant affective states with some unusual activity. And it is impossible to talk definitively about the affections which are involved, so that affective criticism is highly indistinct. (1972: 12)

Even though Ransom was not familiar with Sanskrit poetics, his pioneering statement above brings to one's mind some of the central ideas in Sanskrit poetics which is primarily affective criticism. Ransom is radically different from all the Western or Oriental critics who place emotion at the centre of their criticism. He rejects I.A. Richards' view of aesthetic experience as completely shorn of logic. That Richards and Ransom are diametrically opposed to each other on logic in literature is evident from the following prouncement of the former:

> A poet may distort statement: he may make statements which have logically nothing to do with the subject under treatment; he may, by metaphor or otherwise, present objects for thought which are logically quite irrelevant, he may perpetrate logical *non-sense,* be as trivial or as silly logically, as it is possible to be (518: 5, emphasis added).

This statement of Richards brings him close to Derrida and takes him as far from Ransom as possible. For Ransom, literature renders a kind of knowledge which science cannot. In his emphasis on logic in literature, Ransom is at the other extreme from Derrida. But it must be said that howsoever original Ransom's aesthetics may be, one cannot dissociate emotion altogether from aesthetic experience. The world which is provided by images is both emotionally felt and intellectually apprehended.

A has been said above, Sanskrit poetics excludes thought from aesthetic experience, which is out-and-out an emotional experience. In fact, in its emphasis on emotion, Sanskrit poetics outstrips Western romantic criticism. Emotionalism which Ransom decries is present in its extreme form in Sanskrit poetics. The crux of literature, according to Sanskrit critics, is not what goes into the making of it, or what is embodied in it, but what comes out of it to the reader. Hence, so much emphasis on the sensitive reader (*sahriday)* and his visceral response to literature. Expatiating on Anandavardhana's concept of poetry, K. Krishnamoorthy writes:

> In poetry language is used uniquely because the poet endeavours to convey emotions, moods and feelings in addition to mere facts and actions. Even such hard and dry things like stones and bones become associated with some mental feeling like anguish; and therefore even in seemingly *rasa*-less passages of poetry, a perceptive and sensitive reader will experience some shade or the other of *rasādi.* (XXX: VI)

Facts and actions alongwith feelings and emotions are what the poet seeks to convey, but what the reader receives from his poetry is emotional experience. This is reinforced by V.K. Chari's comment on what goes into and what comes out of literature according to Sanskrit critics:

> The basic assumption of the *rasa* theory is that the object of poetry is not to convey information about the world or simply to affirm facts but to exhibit the feeling responses produced in people by the objects and facts of the world. (298)

This observation on Sanskrit poetics establishes that thought is absent from what the reader receives from literature as a result of his 'feeling responses'. But the fact of the matter is that what comes to the reader in the course of his aesthetic experience is not just emotion but a blend of thought and emotion with the preponderance of the latter. This is also the crux of Eliot's theory of the unification of sensibility.

At the other end of the spectrum, when the New Critics postulate literature as knowledge, it is not the dry knowledge of science which results from abstract cogitation, but the knowledge which comes out of aesthetic experience. John Crowe Ransom has already been discussed in detail. To Cleanth Brooks and Austin Warren, 'poetry enables us to know what it 'feels like' to be alive in this world'.(9) There is a difference between 'feel' and 'feel like'. In the world, we feel when we are face to face with worldly phenomenon, but in the domain of literature, we experience imaginatively created objects through imaginative enactment, which make us visualize them as they exist in the real world, though they are physically absent: we feel 'as if' the objects were before us. Thus, we experience in literature a much wider world than we are familiar with in real life.

As is evident from the foregoing discussion, literature is not without logic and, therefore, Derrida's argument that language is literature and as such there is no language which can convey logic or truth is untenable. Literature and non-literature have their distinct identities. The former is predominantly emotional with logic in the secondary place, while the latter is predominantly logical with emotion in the secondary place.

We have discussed what is in literature as its content and what the reader gets out of it. The arguments marshalled here run contrary to deconstructive postulates. Deconstructionists do no gainsay that thought, emotion and aesthetic experience exist but their view of these terms in the literary context is radically different. As they do not distinguish between philosophy and literature, they discern thought in literature and emotion in philosophy. Both literature and philosophy or, to be more precise, 'literary' and 'philosophical' are placed by Derrida in quotation marks to give the impression that he views them differently from what has generally been assumed. Both thought and emotion are present in the two disciplines but thought is alogical or illogical and emotion unbridled pleasure.

In literary criticism, there are two distinct approaches to thought. At one end, we have Sidney and Richards who are of the opinion that thought in literature is not logical and at the other end, are critics like Ransom and Winters who find in literature a logic which is essentially the same as logic outside literature. But none of the literary critics has said that logic in literature is countered by the contrary logic resulting in what Derrida calls aporia which is, in the words of M.H. Abrams, an 'insuperable deadlock, a 'doublebind' of incompatible or contradictory meanings which are undecidable.' (58). Which is to say that we cannot choose any one meaning as the right one as it is contradicted by the opposite meaning. This is not always true.

As regards emotion, 'philosophic' emotion both in nature and scope, is not different from 'literary' emotion. The term that Derrida has used for this pleasure is *jouissance,* meaning ecstasy which has sexual connotations. Of deconstructive reading as distinct from conventional reading, Derrida writes:

> Deconstruction perhaps has the effect, if not the mission, of liberating forbidden *jouissance* ... . It is perhaps this *jouissance* which most irritates the all-out adversaries of 'deconstruction'. Who, moreover, blame those they call the 'deconstructionists for depriving them of their habitual delectation in the reading of the great works or the rich treasures of tradition and simultaneously for being too playful, for taking too much pleasure, for saying what they like for their own pleasure, etc. (61)

The ecstasy which the reader experiences when completely united with the text is akin to the consummation of sexual pleasure. Roland Barthes has elaborated on this point in his *The Pleasure of the Text*, where he argues that the readerly text which has an object renders pleasure whereas the writerly text without an object provides ecstasy. As the latter is without an object, its meaning which is polysemous is not directed to a centre but disseminates in multiple directions which often clash with each other. Since the burden of a centre, which imposes discipline, is missing, the reader gets full freedom to enjoy the text the way he wants: it is like a sexual body which does not observe any norms when it comes to enjoyment.

Once we deny that the text, literary or otherwise, generates meanings which are uncontrolled and uncontrollable and that the aesthetic experience and the philosophic emotion are one and the same thing, Derrida's concept of both thought and emotion will be invalidated. The is what has been attempted here. A literary text is both similar to and different from other texts. It is similar in the sense that the experience that goes into the making of a literary text is the experience of our life but its rendering in artistic form makes it different. Once rendered artistically, it becomes everyone's experience which is generated without external stimuli. Logic in literature also has a double character. It cannot be subjected to questioning as it is not the dry logic of philosophy or science but its emotional equivalent but it is questioned when it becomes absurd and completely illogical as the 'suspension of disbelief' breaks and the questioning faculty becomes operative.

Literary critics' understanding of literature and literariness is much better than Derrida's who fails to appreciate the nature of experience that goes into a literary construct. Experience in literature is not without logic and as such the postmodernists' (read deconstructionists') rejection of reason in all writings, because they are no different from literature, stands refuted.

Note

1. The title of M.H. Abrams's book is itself highly suggestive and points to the distinction that he makes between classicism and romanticism on the basis of the metaphors for the mind. For details, see chapter II, 'Imitation and the Mirror' and chapter III, 'Romantic Analogues of Art and Mind' in *The Mirror and the Lamp* (London: Oxford University Press, 1979).

Works Cited

Abrams, M.H. *A Glossary of Literary Terms.* Orlando: Harcourt Brace, 1999.

Anandavardhana. *Dhvanyaloka*, trans. and ed. K. Krishnamoorthy. Delhi: Motilal Banarsidass, 1982.

Brooks, Cleanth and Warren, R.P. *Understanding Poetry*. New York: Holt, Rinchart, and Winston, 1976.

Chari, V.K. *Sanskrit Criticism*. Delhi: Motilal Banarsidass, 1993.

Coleridge, S.T. *Biographia Literaria,* ed. J. Shawcross. London: Oxford University Press, 1962. Vol. II.

Derrida, Jacques. *Acts of Literature*, ed. Derek Attridge. London: Routledge, 1991.

Eliot, T.S. *Selected Essays.* London: Faber and Faber, 1951.

K. Krishnamoorthy. Introduction, *Dhvanyaloka of Anandavardhana*. Delhi: Motilal Banarsidass, 1982.

Leavis, F.R. *Revaluation*. Harmondsworth: Penguin Books, 1964.

——. Compiled by. *A Selection from Scrutiny.* Cambridge: Cambridge University Press, 1968. Vol. 1.

MacLeish, Archibald. *Poetry and Experience.* Harmondsworth: Penguin Books, 1965.

Ransom, John Chowe. 'Criticism as Pure Speculation'. *Essays in Modern Criticism.* ed. R.B. West, New York: Rinehart, 1952.

——. *The World's Body.* Baton Rouge: Louisiana University Press, 1968.

——. *Beating the Bushes.* New York: New Directions, 1972.

Richards, I.A. 'Science and Poetry'. *Criticism* ed. Mark Schorer, M.J. Miles, G. Mekenzie. New York: Harcourt Brace, 1948.

Winters, Yvor. *In Defence of Reason.* Chicago: The Swallow Press, 1937.

Wordsworth, William. 'Preface to *Lyrical Ballads,*' *English Critical Texts,* ed. D.J. Enright and Ernst de Chickera. Delhi: Oxford University Press, 1975.

CHAPTER 7

How Literary is Literary Language?

Stanley Fish, one of the pioneers of reader-response criticism, has questioned the existence of an independent literary language, and denied any line of demarcation between ordinary and literary language in his widely acclaimed essay, 'How Ordinary is Ordinary Language?' He says that his intent in the essay is to

> challenge ordinary language/literary language distinction first by pointing out that it impoverishes both the norm and its supposed deviation, and, secondly, by denying that literature as a class of utterances is identified by formal properties. (97)

Fish is of the opinion that there is only one language which becomes ordinary or literary depending on the reading conventions employed by the reader. He made an interesting experiment in his class at the State University of New York at Buffalo. He wrote the names of half a dozen linguists in the shape of a tree and told his students that what they saw on the board was a religious poem. Applying to the poem the reading strategies of a religious poem, they discovered in those proper names the deeper meanings which would not have occurred to them if they knew that they were the names of the well-known linguists. Richard Ohmann's surname became a source of interesting meanings. It was interpreted as 'Omen' as the poem dealt with foreshadowing and prophesy, 'Oh Man', as it dealt with man's relation with God, and 'Amen', the right conclusion to a religious poem dealing with God's mercy and love.

Fish is not alone in maintaining a one language/two manifestations theory. Jonathan Culler, another reader-response critic, expresses an identical view in his *Structuralist Poetics* and elsewhere. 'The fact that a text is a poem', he writes, 'is not the necessary result of its linguistic properties and attempts to base a theory of poetry on an account of the specific properties of the language of a poem seem doomed to failure.' (162) Like Fish, he tries his theory on a sentence which anyone can use in his day-to-day conversation: 'Yesterday, I went into town and bought a lamp.' Arranged as a poem and examined in the light of reading strategies and conventions of poetry, simple words in the sentence—yesterday, lamp, bought—take on deeper significance and start yielding deeper meanings.[1]

Both Fish and Culler believe in two distinct manifestations of the same language, one ordinary and the other literary. The two-language theory which was first propounded by the Russian formalists and avowedly held by the Anglo-American new critics, has been challenged by the two reader-response critics. Derrida goes a step further and stridently asserts that there is only one language which is literary. Whatever characteristics we identify in literary language, he argues, are also discernible in the so-called ordinary language. Hence, his conclusion that 'there is no assured essence or existence of literature.' (73) Derrida comes strikingly close to Fish and Culler when he says that the difference between literature and non-literature is the difference in attitude and 'a set of objective rules' that govern reading experience:

> Without suspending the transcendent reading but by changing one's attitude with regard to the text, one can always reinscribe in a literary space any statement—a newspaper article, a scientific theorem, a snatch of conversation. There is, therefore, a literary *functioning* and a literary *intentionality,* experience rather than an essence of literature (natural or a historical. (45)

However, there is a difference between Fish and Culler, on the one hand, and Derrida, on the other. The former not only believe that literariness is not inherent in the text but generated by the reader's 'attitude' and 'a set of objective rules' that he employs in his reading, they also demonstrate how it is done in practice and set forth those norms and rules. At any rate, all the three maintain that any piece of writing can be transformed into literature.

In the present chapter, I argue against both the reader-response critics and the deconstructionists. I cannot lend credence to the reader-response critical position that literariness is generated by the reader nor can I accept the deconstructionist postulate that all language is literary. Literariness and literary meaning are generated jointly by the author and the reader and literary language differs from ordinary language not in kind but in degree.

The question in the title of this essay, or, for that matter, the title of Fish's essay is difficult to answer. It is well-nigh impossible to draw a clear line of demarcation between ordinary and literary language or to answer when and where ordinary language becomes literary language. This explains why the Russian formalists and the New Critics simply admitted the existence of two languages without bothering about the borderline. Any attempt to make a strict division of language into ordinary and literary is domed to failure. The terms used by the Russian formalists and the Prague structuralists—familiar/defamiliarized, standard/foregrounded, automatic/deautomatized—indicate predominance, not exclusion. The difference between the two languages is relative, not absolute, which is in tune with what we experience in life. Can we draw a strict line between a good person and a bad person, or between a good governance and a bad governance, or between good and bad in any category of things or persons. Absolute differences are a chimera but if we abandon differences altogether, there will be a chaos. We should admit that there are two languages with their predominant, not exclusive features and that there are some overlappings.

The language of literature employs certain devices like metaphor, symbol, metonymy, myth, etc. which are either absent or only marginally present or present in their dead forms outside literature. S.T. Coleridge, the great romantic critic, introduced a broad term called image which subsumed all the literary devices premised on comparison. In the twentieth century, the term became so popular that a number of scholars and critics studied in detail the use of imagery in individual writers and texts.[2] C.D. Lewis, an important poet of the 1930s, wrote a book on *The Poetic Image* and Frank Kermode, an eminent scholar, titled one of his major works *The Romantic Image.* Metaphor and symbol were the important components of the image.

Coleridge's account of the image which is a product of the writer's creative imagination is reckoned his major contribution to literary criticism. His influence on the modern critics was so decisive that S.E. Hyman went to the extent of saying that 'Coleridge's *Biographia Literaria* published in 1817 is almost the Bible of modern criticism.'(13) Sometimes the term metaphor has been used by modern critics in place of image and praised like Coleridge praised image. Cleanth Brooks, an important New Critic, describes modern criticism as a 'rediscovery of metaphor, a full commitment to metaphor.'(729) The importance of metaphor was first discovered by Coleridge and modern critics have rediscovered and reasserted it.

Coleridge's theory of Imagination is the source of significant literary devices which are often used in critical discussions. His Imagination is a major paradigm shift in Western criticism. As the emphasis shifted from the external reality in the neo-classical age to the poet's thought and emotion in the Romantic period, devices like metaphor, image and symbol were required to express his inner world.

Coleridge's distinction between imagination and fancy has been found exceedingly useful in literary discussions. It is his imagination which is at the back of Richard's theory of Value and Eliot's theory of the unification of sensibility.[3] The main distinction between imagination and fancy is that the former is organic, creative and functional, while the latter is mechanical, reproductive and decorative.

Both imagination and fancy employ images with the difference that the images which are the product of Imagination are charged with layers of meaning, whereas those which are spawned by fancy simply yoke together the tenor and the vehicle, to use I.A. Richards's terms, because of some superficial similarity between them. Coleridge cites the following lines from Shakespeare's 'Venus and Adonis' as an illustration of his imagination:

> Look! how a bright star shooteth from the sky
> So glides he in the night from Venus's eyes.

> And offers the following comments:

> How many images and feelings are here brought together without effort and without discord—the beauty of Adonis, the rapidity of his flight, the yearning yet helplessness of the enamoured gazer,—while shadowy ideal character is thrown over the whole. (220–21)

I.A. Richards, in his book-length study of Coleridge on Imagination, has further commented on Shakespeare's lines to bring out subtle implications of the individual words:

> The separable meanings of each word, Look! (our surprise at the meteor, here at his flight), star (a light giver, an influence, a remote and uncontrollable thing), shooteth (the sudden irremediable portentous fall or death of what has been a guide, a destiny), sky (the source of light and now of ruin), glides (not rapidity only, but fatal ease too), in the night (the darkness of the scene and of Venus's world now)—all these separable meanings are here brought into one. (83)

Both Coleridge and Richards demonstrate how a product of Imagination conveys clusters of meanings. This is the beauty of literary language which is created by the writer and appreciated by the competent reader (Jonathan Culler) or *sahriday* (Sanskrit poetics).

Unlike imagination, fancy employs images superficially and mechanically. Coleridge cites the following lines from Shakespeare's 'Venus and Adonis' as an example of fancy:

> Full gently now she takes him by the hand
> A lily prisoned in a gaol of snow
> Or an ivory in an alabaster band,
> So white a friend engirts so white a foe.

Both Adonis's and Venus's hands are white and so are the objects to which they are compared. On the one hand is the white hand of Adonis compared to lily and ivory and on the other, the white hand of Venus compared to 'a gaol of snow' and 'alabaster band'. There is only a superficial similarity here between the tenor and the vehicle, which does not convey any deeper implications. These images, to cite Coleridge, 'have no connection, natural or moral, but are yoked together by the poet by means of some accidental coincidence.' (Qtd. in Richards, 77) When metaphors are employed in non-literary writings, they are either dead metaphors as in 'legs of a table' which go unnoticed or like the images of Fancy whose metaphorcity does not go beyond the surface.

I have discussed Coleridge at some length to demonstrate how image, which includes metaphor, operates at different levels and how there are differences in the nature and function of imagery not only between literature and non-literature but in the same literary form. Coleridge makes critical discriminations which contrast sharply with the sweeping generalizations of Derrida who fails to see any difference between literature and other disciplines.

Metaphors used by the poet worth his salt bring out deeper meanings beneath the surface. These are living metaphors which deviate from convention, force themselves on the reader's attention, make him pause and think and unearth the meanings which are suggested, not stated. When, for example, Eliot compares the evening to 'a patient etherized on the table' in 'The Love Song of J. Alfred Prufrock' or the human heart to the engine of a taxi in *The Waste Land* or when W.B. Yeats compares an old man to 'a tattered coat upon a stick' in 'Sailing to Byzantium', or when Ezra Pound compares the faces of the people coming out of a metro station to 'petals on a dead black bough' in 'In a Station of the Metro', the image brings out layers of meaning through the analogy between the tenor and the vehicle. It is such metaphors which characterize a work of literature and mark it off from non-literature.

Besides metaphor which in its wider sense subsumes simile, symbol is an important literary device which is employed in literary writings. And symbol, which plays such an important role in literature, is not taken into account by Derrida whose exclusive focus is on metaphor.

Suggested meaning which comes out of a symbol can be looked upon as an exclusive property of literature: it is the source of *rasa* or aesthetic experience which we expect only from a work of art. Ordinary discourse does use metaphors of the nature set out above but it is rare to find symbols in it. Let us take an example from that celebrated twentieth-century poem, *The Waste Land.* In this poem Eliot describes the city of

London where people are rushing over London bridge on the way to their offices:

> Unreal City,
> Under the brown fog of a winter dawn,
> A crowd flowed over London Bridge, so many,
> I had not thought death had undone so many.

'Unreal city' stands for the city of London, the Paris of Baudelaire, the Inferno of Dante as well as any modern city where men have degenerated to an extent that they are no better than corpses. In fact, unreal city is a symbol with multiple allusions. The line 'I had not thought death had undone so many' brings out the hollowness of the modern man by comparing him to those inhabiting Dante's *Inferno* from which the line has been taken. Such symbolic and allusive language is characteristic of literature, which one does not find outside literature.

Lest one should get the impression that it is only in poetry that symbol plays an important role, I must hasten to add that it plays an equally important role in other genres of literature such as drama and fiction. In order to avoid confusion, we must bear in mind that there is a difference between symbol in literature and that in linguistics. In his *The Meaning of Meaning*, a book that falls in the category of semantics, I.A. Richards has used the word symbol in the sense that each word stands for and refers to an object.[4] This is the referentiality of language which was challenged by Ferdinand de Saussure. Here symbol has a fixed meaning which does not suggest anything beyond the object to which it refers. We can distinguish between the literal symbol used in linguistics and the literary symbol used in literature. The word symbol is used here in the latter sense.

In the domain of drama, the plays of Shakespeare are known for their very powerful symbols. The dominant symbols in his plays are storm and music, the former standing for disharmony, disorder, and disturbance and the latter for harmony, order and peace. Broadly speaking, in his tragedies storm and in his comedies music predominates. Storm is so powerful a symbol in Shakespeare's plays that the celebrated Shakespeare scholar, G. Wilson Knight, has done a book-length study of it in *The Shakespearean Tempest.*

The best example of storm in Shakespeare is in *King Lear* where the King's madness which is the worst form of disorder is externalized in the storm. Lear, the King of Britain, has divided his kingdom and given half each to the two eldest daughters who profess, falsely though, that they have unlimited love for him depriving the youngest daughter Cordelia of her share in the kingdom only because she speaks nothing but the truth. When the elder daughters deceive him and do not provide shelter to him and his men, the filial ingratitude hurts him so much that his 'wits begin to turn' and finally he goes mad. His mental disturbance and disorder are reflected in the storm to which he is exposed, as he has no house to live in. The extent to which his mind in perturbed is evident from the following speech of Lear:

> Rumble thy bellyful! Spit fire! Spout rein!
> Nor rain, wind, thunder, fire are my daughters.
> I tax you not, you elements, with unkindness:
> I never gave you kingdom, called you children;
> You own me no subscription: Then let fall
> Your horrible pleasure. Here I stand your slave,
> A poor, infirm, weak and despised old man.

But yet I call you servile ministers,
That will with two pernicious daughters join
Your high-engendered battles 'gainst a head
So old and white as this. O, ho! 'tis foul.

(Act III, Scene II, ll. 14–24)

The storm is personified and addressed by Lear. At first he thinks that he has no reason to blame the storm, as he has given him nothing and hence cannot expect obedience from him but later believes that the storm has joined hands with the two ungrateful daughters in torturing him. How beautifully Lear's state of mind is brought out in the above passage! Such powerful language we shall not find outside literature.

Music as symbolic of love and harmony is significantly present in Shakespeare's mature comedies like *Twelfth Night* and *The Tempest.* Love and marriage are the central theme of a Shakespearean comedy and both are best expressed by the symbol of music. Interestingly enough, in the above comedies the storm becomes instrumental in the meeting of the lovers and their marriage. Such literary language as we find in Shakespeare's plays, though not an altogether new language, is very different from ordinary language.

I have discussed at some length the symbols of storm and music in Shakespeare's plays in order to establish that literature, in its use of literary devices, particularly symbol, is not the same kind of writing as non-literature. Who can say that a Shakespeare's play is similar to Saussure's *Course in General Linguistics* which Derrida has subjected to a deconstructive analysis?

In literary discussions, symbol is looked upon as the finest literary device, superior to metaphor, simile and allegory.

Deconstructionists have idealized allegory so much so that Paul de Man has called one of his major works *Allegories of Reading.* But S.T. Coleridge, one of the finest European critics, dismisses allegory as a product of Fancy and considers symbol a product of his secondary or literary imagination. Distinguishing between allegory and symbol, Coleridge writes:

> An allegory is but a translation of abstract notions into a picture-language, which is itself nothing but an abstraction from objects of the senses, the principal being more worthless even than its phantom proxy, both alike unsubstantial, and the former shapeless to boot. On the other hand, a symbol ... is characterised by a translucence of the especial in the individual, or of the general in the especial, or of the universal in the general. Above all, by the translucence of the eternal through and in the temporal, it always partakes of reality which it renders intelligible, and while it enunciates the whole, abides itself as a living part in that unity, of which it is the representative. (25)

Coleridge believes that in allegory there is a comparison between two objects, but they lie so apart that the one appears to be nothing more than a translation of the other. Both the principal and the proxy, or, in other words, the object described and the idea represented by it become 'unsubstantial', particularly the former, as it has no independent shape or significance. On the contrary, symbol unites the symbolic object and the symbolized thought into one with the result that one can see through it what it stands for. The word 'translucence' in the above citation in highly significant. Translucence is a state between transparency and opacity. The eternal idea lurking behind the temporal object is neither transparent nor opaque but translucent. It is a twilight condition in which we partly see and partly imagine.

Symbols are used in the novel as well, which is generally viewed as the most realistic of all literary forms. The psychological novel which makes use of the stream-of-consciousness technique is also known as the lyrical novel where symbol, as in lyrical poetry, plays a pivotal role. Delineating as it does the inner workings of the human mind, it has to fall back upon symbols to give form to the fleeting impressions.

James Joyce's *Ulysses* is by common consent the finest psychological novel in English. It is significant to note that Ulysses, after whom the novel is titled, is not the eponymous hero of the novel; in fact, he is not even a character but only a myth derived from Homer's *Odyssey* and used as a symbol. By lending the Greek myth symbolic significance, Joyce generates a congeries of fresh meanings which characterize literary languae. In the novel, he is represented by Leopard Bloom, an ordinary middle class advertising canvasser who wanders through the streets of Dublin just as Ulysses does on his way back to Ithaca after the battle of Troy is fought and won. Joyce describes what goes on in the mind of Bloom in the course of a particular day, the 16th June 1904 as he passes from one place to another in Dublin. His wife Molly Bloom represents Ulysses's wife Penelope and Stephen Dedalus, whom he meets at the end of the day and whom he identifies as his lost son, represents Ulysses's son, Telemachus. These myths from Homer's epic are used as symbols. Bloom, the comic equivalent of his mythical prototype, who puts up with all kinds of humiliations including the infidelity of his wife and as such is as far removed from the heroic Ulysses as possible, stands for the modern man.

Even in the essay form we find at times prose which is radically different from ordinary prose. I have in mind particularly the prose of Sir Thomas Browne and Charles Lamb, which is highly allusive, rich in rhythm, shot through with living metaphors and symbols. The following extract from Charles Lamb's famous essay 'In Praise of Chimney Sweepers' is an apt example of literary prose:

> I reverence these young Africans of our own growth—these almost clergy imps, who sport their cloth without assumption; and from their little pulpits (the tops of chimneys), in the nipping air of a December morning, preach a lesson of patience to mankind.

The author's sympathy for the young African boys working as chimney sweepers verges on reverence. The expression 'of our own growth' points to the fact that Africans were brought to the West as slaves and given the derogatory sobriquet of 'negro'. As they are young, they are compared to 'clergy imps' who wear their own dirty clothes dotted with dust particles from chimneys with the same feeling that clergymen feel when they wear their impeccably clean white gowns. This comparison is significant, as the chimney sweepers teach from the chimney tops the same lesson of patience to mankind as the clergymen do from the pulpits with the difference that they do it without any feeling of self-righteousness and embody the patience that they preach and to that extent they are superior to the clergymen. The entire essay is highly allusive, as it refers to several writers and works such as Shakespeare, Hogarth, Milton and the Bible. The kind of prose that Lamb writes in this essay is very different from ordinary prose that we read in newspapers and works of non-literary disciplines like philosophy, history and linguistics.

It is generally believed that the language of realistic fiction comes close to ordinary prose, which is only partly true. Roman Jakobson, the Russian formalist, has placed the language of literature at the opposite poles of metaphor and metonymy, the former predominant in poetry, particularly lyrical poetry, and the latter predominant in fiction, particularly realistic fiction. These are literary devices that distance literary language from ordinary language and literature from non-literature. Whereas a great deal of reading material is available on metaphor, very little has been written on metonymy.

Using Saussure's distinction between paradigmatic and syntagmatic organization of words, Jakobson argues that metaphor is based on similarity and metonymy on contiguity. Of metonymy, he writes:

> Following the path of contiguous relationship, the realist author metonymically digresses from the plot to the atmosphere and from the chracter to the setting in space and time. (57)

Jakobson gives two examples from Tolstoy: the focus on the heroine's handbag in *Anna Karenina* and on the 'hair on the upper lip' and 'bare shoulders' of the female characters in *War and Peace.* This movement from the character to the items closely associated with her metonymically conveys what ordinary prose does not. I cite as an instance of the shifting of focus from the character to the setting an extract from the celebrated Indian novel in English, *The God of Small Things* by Arundhati Roy:

> It was raining when Rahel came back to Ayemenem. Slanting silver ropes slammed into loose earth, ploughing it

> up like gunfire. The old house on the hill wore its steep, gabled roof pulled over its ears like a low hat. The walls, streaked with moss, had grown soft, and bulged a little with dampness that seeped up from the ground. The wild, overgrown garden was full of the whisper and scurry of small lives. In the undergrowth a rat snake rubbed itself against a glistening stone. Hopeful yellow bullfrogs cruised the scummy pond for mates. A drenched mongoose flashed across the leaf-strewn driveway.

Where shall we find this language outside literature? This is the world-disclosing language of literature that Habermas talks about.[5] Rahel has returned to Ayemenem after a gap of 23 years and in the meantime the entire surrounding has changed. The novel gives a graphic account of the surrounding with minute details of small things. The movement from the character to the setting that Jakobson speaks of is best illustrated here.

Sanskrit poetics is a mine of information on the nature of literature as distinct from non-literature. It is often presumed that *rasa dhvani* (also referred to as *dhvani)* as propounded by Anandavardhana in his *Dhvanyaloka* is the ultimate criterion evolved in Sanskrit poetics to mark literature off from non-literature. It is argued that *dhvani* alone is enough to generate literariness. But this is far from true, as the examples of *dhvani* can be found in ordinary discourse as well. Let us take the utterance which is so often cited and so extensively discussed as an example of *dhvani*: *Gangayam ghoshah* (a village on the Ganga). Here the literal meaning (*vyachartha)* is obstructed as a village cannot exist on the stream of water. So one takes recourse to indicated meaning (*lakshnartha)* to get the sense that the village is on the bank of the river. But the indication is only an extension of the statement, not a new meaning. From the context one gathers that what the speaker really intends to convey is the idea of sanctity and holiness associated with the river Ganga, the most sacred river for the Hindus. This third meaning is suggestion (*vangyartha)*, which is embodied in the utterance like the soul in the body.

Anandvardhana has said time and again that *dhvani* is neither stated nor indicated but suggested. *Dhvani* is implication as against statement which rests on the denotative property of language and indication which is spawned by metaphors and other figures of speech. Unlike Western theorists, Anandavardhana makes a threefold division of linguistic properties and the meanings that they generate. Western criticism, on the other hand, makes a twofold division: denotation which we find in ordinary language, also called standard or familiar language and connotation or suggestion, the chief characteristic of literary or defamiliarized language generated by devices like metaphor, simile, symbol, personification, consonance, dissonance, etc. Anandavardhana makes a distinction between connotation and suggestion, the former being the explicit and the latter the implicit meaning. To him, metaphor and other figural devices only extend the explicit literal meaning. Metaphor itself is divided into two categories: that which is based on external embellishment and that which has a deeper meaning. This twofold division of metaphor is comparable to Coleridge's distinction between mechanical and organic images produced by fancy and imagination, respectively. A metaphor without a deeper meaning is illustrated in the following lines cited by Anandavardhana:

> Angry or pleased in tears or in smiles
> In whatever state they are caught
> Wanton women *steal* one's heart.

The parallel between stealing someone's heart and stealing someone's valuables does not have any deeper meaning. This parallelism is like the superficial comparison made in Shakespeare's lines quoted by Coleridge as an example of fancy. Metaphor with some deeper meaning, on the contrary, contributes significantly to the emotive meaning but remains subservient to the explicit meaning. Anandavardhana cites the following lines with his own gloss in the brackets to illustrate the secondary role of suggestion in a figure of speech (a condensed metaphor in this case):

> The twilight (heroine's face) with twinkling star (shining pupils) was illumined (kissed) by the moon (the hero) glowing red (overcome by emotion) so suddenly (with such love) that the entire mass of darkness (black garment) disappearing in the east (slipping even in front), due to illumination (love) was not at all noticed. (21)

Anandavardhana advances the following general observation on the above example:

> It is the explicit meaning alone which appears as prominent and the suggestive sense is only secondary to it. The main subjects of description are the night and the moon. And the behaviour of a heroine and that of a hero are attributed to them (only secondary). (23)

The above example and Anandavardhana's comments make it clear that the suggestion generated by a figure of speech only serves to highlight the denotative meaning.

Anandavardhana makes it clear that suggestion is not expressed but implied. In *Gangayam ghoshah*, the idea of holiness and sanctity is nowhere explicitly expressed but only suggested by the context. Anandavardhana makes a sharp division between the explicit meaning which is the domain of *vyachyarth* (stated meaning) as well as *lakshnartha* (indicated meaning) and the implicit meaning which is the realm of *dhvani* or *vangyartha* (suggested meaning), and he privileges the last over the first two. In underlining suggestion and giving metaphor a secondary place, Anandavardhana's poetics differs from Western theories where metaphor has been foregrounded as a device which generates suggestion. Anandavardhana cites the following lines as an example of suggestion:

> Ramble freely pious man,
> That dog today is killed
> By the fierce lion that dwells
> In Goda river dells.

The explicit meaning of these lines is a 'positive proposal' but what is suggested, though not stated, is a 'prohibition'. The lover wants to tell the priest, who used to impede his dalliance with his beloved, to restrict his movements as a 'fierce lion' is on the prowl in the area. This will give the lover freedom from the priest's interference and he can move freely with the lady he loves. But instead of saying this explicitly, which may have given the priest the impression that the lover was playing a trick on him, he says just the opposite. 'The implicit aspect,' writes Anandavardhana, 'is entirely different from the explicit aspect, and it is found in the words of first rate poets.' (9) In the above example what is suggested takes precedence over what is explicitly stated. In fact, the explicit meaning is not only marginalized but nullified.

For Anandavardhana, *dhvani* is the soul of poetry: it is 'both the quintessence of the works of all first rate poets and the most beautiful principle of poetry.' (7) The crux of great poetry is explained through an analogy. In a lady, individual limbs do contribute to her beauty, but her real charm exceeds the beauty of her individual limbs seen separately. Suggestion in poetry is akin to this charm in a lady. The embellishment of the explicit meaning by the figures of sense as well as the figures of sound are the ornaments of the body, but the real charm of poetry lies in suggestion. Drawing parallelism between the meaning that comes out of a sentence and the suggestion which emerges from an expression, Anandavardhana writes: 'suggested meaning flashes suddenly across the truth-perceiving minds of perceptive critics, when they turn away from the literal meaning.'(19). The suggested meaning as defined by Anandavardhana comes close to James Joyce's epiphany which is 'a sudden sense of radiance and revelation that one may feel while perceiving a common place object.'(Abrams, 80)

Though suggestion transcends literal meaning which characterizes ordinary discourse, it does not discard it. In a significant statement, Anandavardhana says:

> When a suggested sense is apprehended, the expressed sense is not driven away to a distance since the apprehension of the suggested is inseparably occasioned by the apprehension of the expressed. (201)

Anandavardhana takes an analogy. The pot in darkness which is the suggested sense is made visible by the lamplight which is the literal sense but once the pot is revealed, the lamp-light does not disappear, as in its absence the pot will again be in darkness and thus invisible. In a figurative expression, the reader confronts some obstruction, some inconsistency in the literal meaning, which is resolved with the help of indication enshrined in a figure of speech. But there is no such inconsistency in suggestion (*vyanjana)*, as the literal meaning remains intact and suggestion comes out of it in a flash, as in the example already discussed. Suggestion, according to Anandavardhana, characterizes literature as well as distinguishes it from non-literature. If for Western critics metaphor is the soul of literature, for Anandavartdhana it is suggestion. If in the West Coleridge popularized metaphor in the name of image, in the East, it is Anandavardhana who has popularized suggestion. Both Coleridge and Anandavardhana exercised a decisive influence on subsequent critics.

Anyone interested in and idealizing Sanskrit poetics will advance, as Krishna Rayan does,[6] *dhvani* (suggestion or implication) as the exclusive property of literature, which is absent from non-literature. But there is a problem here. Suggestion or implication, as contrasted with statement and indication, is discerned outside literature as well. If *dhvani* is suggestion and suggestion is implication, which is different from indication produced by figures of speech, then we find examples of *dhvani* outside literature, too. We have in English 'implicature' which is used in common parlance when an idea is suggested, not stated. The entry on 'implicature' in *The Concise Oxford English Dictionery*, 10th edition, 2002 is as under:

> Implicature: The action of implying a meaning beyond the literal sense of what is explicitly stated, for example saying *The frame is nice* and implying I *don't like the picture in it.* (712)

How is implicature different from suggestion which is made so much of in Sanskrit poetics? And we must not forget that 'implicature' is not listed in the dictionary as 'formal' or 'literary', which means that it is still used in the day-to-day communication, oral as well as written. This is corroborated by Edward Sapir's observation on the nature of language and the way words convey their meanings in ordinary speech. Arguing that in a certain context words can convey a meaning which is the opposite of what they mean literally, Sapir writes:

> The choice of words in a particular context may convey the opposite of what they mean on the surface. The same external message is differently interpreted according to whether the speaker has this or that psychological status in his personal relations, or whether such primary expressions as those of affection, or anger, or fear may inform the spoken words with a significance which completely transcends their normal value. (10)

How does suggestion help in distinguishing literature from non-literature? The problem, though escaped by conservative scholars of Sanskrit poetics, is fully realized by V.K. Chari in his very comprehensive, critical and perceptive account of Sanskrit poetics in *Sanskrit Criticism*, where he writes:

> Anandavardhana realizes that suggested meanings are adventitious and entirely context dependent ... . All meanings are in fact contextual. So what point is gained by assigning it to a special verbal activity called suggestion? (102)

And, again,

> Moreover, the *dhavani* argument leads to another embarrassment. Since all suggested meaning is contextual meaning, it should follow that all contextual meaning is suggested meaning. But, at this rate, the protagonist of *dhvani* will have to admit that the implication of the most prosaic and trivial sort ... are also stances of poetic suggestion. (103)

Here Chari advances solid objections to *dhvani* as the exclusive property of poetry, and by implication, of all forms of literature. Of course, *dhvani* theorists can answer their opponents saying that *rasa dhvani*, not *dhvani* alone marks literature off from non-literature. But Anandavardhana does not distinguish between the two and throughout *Dhvanyaloka* there is a general impression that one is synonymous with the other. This, in my opinion, is the main weakness of Anandavardhana's poetics, which he could have got over by taking recourse to symbol where the literal meaning on the surface (*abidhartha)* is charged with layers of deeper meaning. Of the two examples of *dhvani* discussed above, the one which is addressed to the priest and where the speaker suggests just the opposite of what he states can be taken as the *dhvani* of ordinary discourse whereas the other example, *Gangayam ghoshah* is an instance of *rasa-dhvani*. What is the difference between the two? In the second example, Ganga becomes a symbol, as it stands for sanctity and holiness whereas the first example is simply an oblique statement suggesting a meaning, which is the opposite of what is stated.

It is surprising that while so many figures of speech are listed and examined in *Dhvanyaloka,* symbol does not figure. We know that in Western criticism, symbol is given pride of place and many a critic has considered it the finest literary device. The importance of symbol was realized during the Romantic phase in England and the Symbolist phase in France. The latter witnessed a long tradition of Symbolist poetry running for over a century from Gerard de Nerval to Paul Valery. Arthur Symons highlighted the importance of symbol in his *Symbolist Movement in Literature.* But Derrida does not seem familiar with the importance of symbol which more effectively than metaphor distinguishes literature from non-literature. The focus of deconstruction is on metaphor, although Derrida and his acolytes have not discussed it in all its aspects as Paul Ricoeur does in *The Rule of Metaphor*. By foregrounding metaphor as an integral part of language, literary as well as non-literary, deconstruction comes to the conclusion that all language is essentially literary and all verbal constructions are literature.

By focusing on the devices other than metaphor such as image, myth and symbol and demonstrating how literary language is different from ordinary language, I have sought to reply to Derrida's sweeping generalization with my critical discrimation. For Derrida, language operates only at one level which is literary, but, in fact, it operates at several levels. Even literary language is not always the same. At one end we have the language of Shakespeare's major plays, while at the other end the language of Dickens's novels. Even in the writings of the same author we find several levels. This is evident if we compare the language of Shakespeare's tragedies with that of his comedies or the language of Wordsworth's *The Prelude* with that of his 'Thorn' or the language of Eliot's *The Waste Land* with that of *The Cocktail Party*.

Derrida affirms that whatever we identify as characteristic of literary language is also discernible outside literature.

If metaphor is the literary device which generates literariness, metaphor, Derrida can reply, is not confined to literature, as it is ubiquitously present in all languages and all disciplines. Deconstruction which is viewed by Derrida as synonymous with literariness informs literature as well as non-literature. This makes the distinction between literary and non-literary language and also literary and non-literary text untenable. At one point Derrida comes close to accepting the distinct identity of literary language when he writes:

> What is the specific difference of literary language in this respect? Does its originality consist in stopping, arresting attention of the excess of language over language. (48)

This 'stopping, arresting attention of the excess of [literary] language over [ordinary] language' is how literature can be defined. But Derrida rejects it and goes on to say:

> In exhibiting, re-marking, giving to be re-marked this excess of language as literature, i.e. an institution which cannot identify itself because it is always in relationship, the relationship with the non-literary. No: for it shows nothing without dissimulating *what* it shows and that it shows it. (48).

One can answer Derrida by saying that some relationship of the literary language with the non-literary cannot be denied but the literary language goes beyond the ordinary language and it is in this 'beyond' that literature can be identified.

Derrida's argument is that there in no exclusive literary language but he cannot deny the big difference in degree, if not in kind, between the language of literature and that of other disciplines like philosophy, history, linguistics, etc. The problem lies in the medium of literature, which is so different from the mediums of the other fine arts. The stone and the chisel which are the medium of the sculptor, and the brush, the paint, and the canvas which constitute the medium of the painter are not shared by the common people, but this is not true of the medium of literature, which is also the medium of expression for ordinary people. However, the same medium of language takes different forms in literature and non-literature and the differences between them are engendered by the devices which have already been discussed. Derrida will reply that these devices one comes across outside literature as well. Even so, there is a difference: they are predominant in literature whereas in non-literature, they are either absent or marginal.

Notes

1. For Jonathan Culler's comments on the sentence see his 'Linguistics as a Model for Poetics', *Twentieth Century American Criticism: Interdisciplinary Approaches*, ed. Rajnath (New Delhi: Arnold-Heinemann, 1977), pp. 99–100.
2. Some major publications in the field are Caroline Spurgeon, *Shakespeare's Imagery* (Cambridge: At the University Press, 1952), Florence Marsh, *Wordsworth's Imagery* (New Haven: Yale University Press, 1952), R.H. Fogle, *The Imagery of Keats and Shelley* (Hamden: Archon Books, 1962), R.B. Heilman, *This Great Stage: Image and Structure in King Lear* (Seattle: University of Washington Press, 1962), and Rajnath, *Nature Imagery of the Major Romantic Poets* (Varanasi: The Oriental Book Society, 1965; Delhi: Doaba House, 2014).
3. See Rajnath, 'Richard's Theory of Value in Relation to Coleridge's Theory of Imagination,' *Essays in Criticism* (Delhi:

Doaba House, 2004) pp. 86–91, and 'Introduction', *T.S. Eliot: Selected Essays* (Delhi: Doaba Publications, 2008), p. xvi.

4. In his *The Meaning of Meaning* (London: Routledge, 1952), Richards makes a perceptive distinction between the symbolic use of words to make statements and their emotive use to express or excite feeling and attitude. Elsewhere in his writings, Richards has replaced 'symbolic' with 'scientific'.
5. See Jûrgen Habermas, 'Levelling the Genre Distinction between Philosophy and Literature,' *The Derrida-Habermas Reader*, ed. Lasse Thomassen (Edinburgh: Edinburgh University Press, 2006).
6. See Krishna Rayan, *Suggestion and Statement in Poetry* (London: The Athlone Press, 1972) and *Sahitya: A Theory* (New Delhi: Sterling, 1991)

Works Cited

Abrams. M.H. *A Glossary of Literary Terms.* Orlando: Harcourt Brace, 1999.

Anandavardhana. *Dhvanyaloka.* tr. and ed. K. Krishnamoorthy. Delhi: Motilal Banarasidass, 1993.

Brooks, Cleanth. 'Irony as a Principle of Structure', *Literary Opinion in America,* ed. M.D. Zabel. New York: Harper Torchbooks, 1962.

Chari, V.K. *Sanskrit Criticism.* New Delhi: Motilal Banarasidass, 1993.

Coleridge, S.T. 'The Statesman's Manual'. *The Political Tracts of Wordsworth, Coleridge and Shelley,* ed. R.J. White, London: Cambridge University Press, 1953.

Coleridge, S.T. *Lectures and Notes on Shakespeare* and *Other English Poets.* ed. T. Ash. London: G. Bells, 1908.

Culler, Jonathan. *Structuralist Poetics.* Ithaca: Cornell University Press. 1981.

Derrida, Jacques, *Acts of Literature*, ed. Derek Attridge. London: Routledge, 1991.

Fish, Stanley. *Is there a Text in this Class*? Cambridge, Mass.: Harvard University Press, 1980.

Hyman, S.E. *The Armed Vision*. New York: Vintage Books, 1955.

Jakobson, Roman. 'The Metaphoric and Metonymic Poles.' *Modern Criticism and Theory*, ed. David Lodge. Delhi: Pearson, 2004.

Richards, I.A. *Coleridge on Imagination*. London: Routledge, 1968.

Sapir, Edward. *Culture, Language and Personality*, ed. David G. Mandelbaum. Berkley: University of California Press, 1949.

CHAPTER 8

Critical Practice

Reading Derrida Reading *Romeo and Juliet*

Romeo and Juliet, one of Shakespeare's most popular plays, has especially fascinated structuralists, semioticians and poststructuralists because of the one observation on language in a speech by Juliet:

> What's in a name? That which we call a rose
> By any other name would smell as sweet.
>
> So Romeo would, were he not Romeo call'd
> Retain that dear perfection which he owes
> Without that title (II.ii. 43–47)[1]

This speech impinged so deeply on Umberto Eco, the Italian semiotician, novelist and critic that he wrote out a novel under the title, *The Name of the Rose,* which became a best-seller.

Derrida has subjected *Romeo and Juliet* to a deconstructive analysis using terms like aporia, dissymmetry, disjunction and most importantly, countertime in an essay significantly titled 'Aphorism Countertime.' Aphorism is a term that Derrida has used in contrast to essay which unites disparate ideas into unity: aphorism attempts a kind of dissemination, to use Derrida's own term.

Derrida's central argument that the spatio-temporal time which results in linear action is contradicted by countertime results in not only aporia but a double aporia. Romeo and Juliet fall in love at first sight, but they belong to families, the Montagues and the Capulets, who do not see eye with each other. They first meet at a party organized by Juliet's parents, Mr and Mrs Capulets, where Romeo, a Montague, surreptitiously enters. Interestingly enough, Romeo is already in love with a young woman, Rosaline, who had not responded to his love and Juliet's parents have already chosen a young man, county Paris, for her marriage for which they only need their daughter's consent. Contrary to her parents' expectation, Juliet meets at this party Romeo, an uninvited guest who falls in love with her and she with equal warmth responds.

Here Derrida's countertime asserts its role shattering the dreams of not only Juliet's parents but also the young lovers. Time goes against them in a series of events leading to the banishment of Romeo from Verona to Mantua, the enforced wedding planned for Juliet with Paris, the strategy of Friar Laurence which misfires and the eventual tragic end of the young lovers.

Time in the play, argues Derrida, is a double bind: it unites but it also separates. Time brings Romeo and Juliet together at the party but time also throws them apart. The linear movement of time and space is designed to unite the lovers but the incidents spawned by it including death precludes the very possibility of such a union: the time temporal is undercut by countertime replacing homogeneity with heterogeneity.

Derrida explains the peculiar situation in which the lovers find themselves. Since they are two, they know with absolute certainty that

> Since we are two, we know in an absolutely ineluctable way that one of us will die before the other. One of us will see the other die, one of us will live on, even if only for an instant. One of us, only one of us, will carry the death of the other and the mourning. It is impossible that we should each survive the other (422).

But the impossible happens: each mourns the death of the other and each survives the other. Juliet dies though it is only a temporary death, when Romeo is still alive and Romeo, getting the news of Juliet's death as real, buys poison from an apothecary in Mantua, comes to Verona, opens the tomb of Juliet, kisses her, takes the poison and dies when, in fact, Juliet is still alive. When Juliet wakes from the death-semblance induced by the potion given by the Friar, she discovers Romeo dead, takes the dagger that Romeo had brought with him and stabs herself to death.

The real aporia for Derrida is in the naming. The young lovers wish to jettison their surnames, as they portend problems in their relationship, but at the same time they need them in order to express their feelings. By the prevalent cultural practice it is the husband who retains his surname while the wife takes her husband's name as Montague's and Capulet's wives do. Hence, Juliet wants Romeo to abandon it to become acceptable to her parents and in exchange take the whole of her:

> Romeo, doff thy name
> And for the name, which is no part of thee
> Take all myself.

After all, what's in a name, she asks? Nothing, as without it Romeo is what he is, just as the rose will smell the same even if it is called by another name:

> What's in a name? That which we call a rose
> By any other word would smell as sweet
> So Romeo would, were he not Romeo called
> Retain that dear perfection which he owes
> Without that title. (II. ii. 43–47)

But from another perspective, Romeo loses everything: he loses his identity without which he cannot even tell Juliet who he is: 'By a name/I know not how to tell thee.' (II. ii. 54–55)

Juliet is not selfish. She does not desire only Romeo to give up his surname while she retains her own. She candidly states that if Romeo loves her but does not want to discard his name that he has inherited from his father, she will give up her own surname:

> Deny they father and refuse thy name.
> Or, if thou wilt not, be but sworn by love,
> And I'll no longer be a Capulet. (II. ii. 34–37).

Juliet's demand is at once conceded by Romeo:

> My name, dear saint, is hateful to myself.
> Because it is an enemy to thee. (II. ii. 56–57)

Romeo's name is the only way to disclose his identity but at the same time he reckons it hateful because it is Juliet's enemy. The fact is that the name is also his enemy which brought him close to death. Derrida comments on the ambivalence in the naming:

> She wants the death of Romeo. She will have it. The death of his name ('Tis but they name that is my enemy'),certainly, the death of 'Romeo,' but they will not he able to get free from their name, they know this without knowing it. She declares war on 'Romeo,' on his name, in his name, she will win this war only on the death of Romeo himself. Himself? Who? Romeo. But 'Romeo' is not Romeo. Precisely. She wants the death of 'Romeo,' Romeo dies, 'Romeo' lives on. (426)

There are two Romeos, Romeo, the physical entity and 'Romeo', the name. It is possible to separate the two, as the relation between the two is arbitrary like the one between the rose and the word 'rose'. It is possible not only in the case of Romeo but any name including Juliet's. But the irony is not only that they cannot dissociate themselves from their names, they do not wish to, as they need them for the expression of their love. The name continues even after the death of the person, as Romeo is known by his name after his physical death and Juliet by her. The contradictory attitudes to naming generates undecidability which is the crux of Derrida's aporia.

Derrida finds in the play a double aporia. Romeo agrees, as demanded by Juliet, to exchange his name for the whole of Juliet. He loses nothing but he gains everything. Derrida summarizes Romeo's opinion followed by his own comment.

> I lose nothing in taking you at your word and take absolutely all of you. In truth, and they both know the truth

> of aphorism, he will lose everything. They will lose everything in this aporia, this double aporia of the proper name. (429).

In this double aporia Romeo gains everything but he also loses everything and Juliet too loses everything in losing the identity of Romeo. But who is Romeo, the man or the name, perhaps both, or perhaps difficult to decide. This movement from the name to 'not name' and back to the name is a double aporia. This is also a double aporia in the sense that it is a condition of undecidability for both Romeo and Juliet.

Does Derrida do justice to Shakespeare's masterpiece? Not in my opinion. In the first place, he forces the text into a deconstructive analysis and finds out aporia where none exists. We know that time can be good or bad depending on the situation. Time is good when Romeo and Juliet fortuitously meet at the party where neither has expected the other, and it is bad for both when the letter from the Friar does not reach Romeo in time. Naming, like timing, can both help and hinder. It is evident in a country like India where the caste system is so dominant. Surname which indicates one's caste can help and get one favours but it can also cause hindrance.

As regards death and survival, three situations are possible. In the first, both the persons die simultaneously and none survives to mourn the death of the other; in the second, the two persons die by turn and one mourns the death of the other; in the third, someone is presumed to be dead and his death is mourned but he is actually alive. Where does the death of Romeo and Juliet stand? The temporary death-like semblance induced by the Friar's potion should not be reckoned death. The audience as well as the Friar know this fact. Juliet dies her physical death only after the death of Romeo. Romeo dies before Juliet and he mourns her death only because of his ignorance. Thus, the physical death of Romeo and Juliet comes by turn, not simultaneously and one dying because of the death of the other is a common place in life as in literature.

Derrida's enforced deconstructive reading of *Romeo and Juliet* distracts our attention from the central theme of the play. For a literary critic there is much more in the play than timing and naming. I wish to demonstrate the difference between a philosopher's and a literary critic's response to the same text. Harold Bloom, with a doubtful relationship with the deconstructionists, has done an extended study of *Romeo and Juliet* in his *Shakespeare: The Invention of the Human.* Interestingly enough, he does not even cite Juliet's speech on the relationship between the name and the object, the speech which is made so much of by Derrida who cites it twice and makes it the fulcrum of his discussion of the play. Bloom focuses on the theme of love and death, pays very little attention to the timing and no attention to the naming. In fact, a single page of Bloom's book, p. 89, tells more about the play than Derrida's longish discussion running into 18 pages. Two comments on the play by Bloom made on the page under reference are given below:

> *Romeo and Juliet* is unmatchable in Shakespeare and in the world's literature, as a vision of an uncompromising mutual love that perishes of is own idealism and intensity. (89)

> It is easier to see the vividness of Mercutio and the Nurse than it is to absorb and sustain the erotic greatness of Juliet and the heroic effort of Romeo to approximate her sublime state of being in love. (89)

In these two extracts Blooms tells us about the nature of love and the level of characterization. Love depicted in the play is unique in world literature as the lovers perish not only because of the intensity of love but also idealism. They could have run away from Verona to Mantua or any other country and lived there a happy married life but they go neither against the law nor against their parents.

In the second extract above, Bloom is differentiating between Mercurto and the Nurse on the one hand and Juliet and Romeo on the other. For the audience it is easier to comprehend the obscenity and crudity of the former than the sublimity of Juliet and the heroism of Romeo. It is difficult for them to understand that there can be something called 'erotic greatness' which is equivalent to 'sublime state of being' and 'heroic effort' which has nothing to do with physical strength. But so it is in *Romeo and Juliet.* Eroticism can be vulgar as it is in the case of Mercutio and the Nurse, but it can be sublime as in the case of Juliet. Heroism can be a show of physical strength which Romeo displays in slaying Tybalt and Paris but what is more important is cultural heroism which is manifested in Romeo's response to Juliet's love. To elaborate on Bloom's observation on the erotic greatness of Juliet, I take a couple of examples. If Romeo gives up his name, says Juliet, he will remain the same in all the parts of his body because the name is

> nor hand, nor foot,
> nor arm, nor face, *nor any other part*
> *belonging to a man.* (II. ii. 40–42, italics mine).

The italicized portion hints at eroticism without explicitly stating it. The unmentioned part of the body is also reckoned unmentionable by her. Compare this with the crude Mercutio's use of the word 'demesnes', i.e. domains which lie adjacent to her 'quivering thigh' (II., i, 19–20). When Juliet says that in exchange for his name Romeo can take the whole of herself or 'take all myself', eroticism is implied, just as it is when in response to Romeo's, 'Wilt thou leave me so unsatisfied?' Juliet says, 'What satisfaction canst thou have tonight?' (II, ii. 125–26). The maximum that they have gone so far is kissing each other and here Juliet not only does not resist, she cooperates. They spend a night together after their marriage before Romeo leaves for Mantua. This was their brief honeymoon when presumably they had physical relationship. They appear fully gratified after their night together, although none in the two families knows about it. It is evident from their speeches that they were up all night and they are very unwilling to part at dawn.

Bloom's last two sentences on the page take the comparisons beyond the play:

> Shakespeare, at this point of his career, may have underestimated his burgeoning power, because Mercutio and the Nurse go on seducing audiences, readers, directors and critics. Their verbal exuberances make them forerunners of Touchstone and Jacques, rancid ironists but also the eloquent villains, Iago and Edmund. (89)

Much light is shed on the characters in the play and also, by comparison, those in the other plays of Shakespeare. *Romeo and Juliet* is a love tragedy and as such contains the elements of comedy as well as tragedy with a tragic end. Of the characters that Mercutio and the Nurse foreshadow, Touchstone and Jacques figure in Shakespeare's celebrated comdey *As you Like*

It, while Iago and Edmund appear in Shakespeare's major tragedies *Othello* and *King Lear,* respectively.

We have seen the difference between Derrida and Bloom on *Romeo and Juliet* and there is little doubt that a student of literature will side with Bloom rather than Derrida. Trained as a philosopher, Derrida sees only the philosophical dimension of the play and the deconstructive aporia at work in the text. Bloom sees it as a play, a particular kind of play called tragedy, a Shakespearean love tragedy at that, which calls for and receives focus on the literary dimension.

Aristotle, the father of Western criticism and also of Western philosophy, wrote the first treatise on drama. His theory of drama can help us understand *Romeo and Juliet* much better than Derrida's dry philosophical approach. Aristotle has listed six constituents of drama of which four, namely action, character, thought, diction, relate to its internal structure while the two—melody and spectacle—are external factors relating to the theatre. The four internal constituents are arranged in an hierarchical order, i.e. that which comes first is the most important. For him action or plot is the soul of tragedy (read drama). In the Shakespeare oeuvre, action is central to a comedy whereas the character of the hero is at the centre of a tragedy. This is evident from the titles of the plays: comedies are named after aspects of action and the tragedies after the heroes. Love culminating in marriage is the theme of a Shakespearean comedy, while strife and conflict leading ineluctably to death is the theme of a Shakespearean tragedy.

Romeo and Juliet is a unique drama in the Shakespearean corpus. Here love and strife, marriage and death go side by side. This explains why the lovers meet surreptitiously and their marriage is secretly solemnized by Friar Laurence, which only the Nurse is in the know of. Romeo and Juliet are among the strongest of Shakespeare's lovers, whose love is best described by Juliet, though she speaks only for herself, through the analogy of the sea:

> My bounty is as boundless as the sea
> My love as deep, the more I give to thee
> The more I have, for both are infinite. (II.ii. 132–35)

The entire balcony scene from which this citation comes is an evidence of the strong passion of love that the lovers feel for each other. But the irony is that such intense love is always under the shadow of death which finally engulfs it.

Unlike Shakespeare's major tragedies, *Romeo and Juliet* is named after both the hero and the heroine and the relationship between the two is the central theme of the play. The action moves from love to death, although throughout the play the death of Romeo as well as Juliet is narrowly escaped. But for the kindness of Capulet, Romeo would have been killed by Tybalt at the party presumably assisted by others and but for the mercy of the Prince of Verona, he would have been sentenced to death for killing Tybalt. On the other hand, Juliet is being forced by her parents to marry Paris which she can not tolerate and self-slaughter seems to be the only option left for her. The poisonous drink given by the Friar induces temporary death which is taken as real by the others. So, like Romeo, she is always close to death until they finally die.

The play does not have what Aristotle calls the unity of action as tragic and comic elements get mixed up and also there are two secondary streams of action, one which centres on Paris's one-sided love for Juliet, and the other that involves the murder of Mercutio by Tybalt and the murder of Tybalt by Romeo for which he is banished to Mantua. These streams of action do not go separately but intersect with each other as well as the main action, which engenders that organic unity of effect which vindicates Shakespeare's violation of the mechanically imposed dramatic unity of action.

As regards character which is accorded the second place in Aristotle's theory of drama, it is, in fact, the first and foremost constituent of a Shakespearean tragedy while in a Shakespearean comedy it is subservient to action. Aristotle had not seen a dramatic genius like Shakespeare who could write such a wide variety of plays and equally excel in both tragedy and comedy. In *Romeo and Juliet,* action and character are equally important. The two main characters in *Romeo and Juliet* are the eponymous hero and heroine. There are other characters closely associated with them, Mercutio with Romeo and the Nurse with Juliet. Juliet's parents, highly conservative in their belief, fall in another category. County Paris, Romeo's rival in love, is a very common category in literature as in life.

Juliet is more mature, more in control of her emotion than Romeo who can kill someone on the spur of the moment and repent later. After slaying Tybalt, Juliet's cousin, he feels such strong remorse that he tries to kill himself when the Nurse intervenes and snatches his dagger. On the other hand, Juliet makes only one emotional outburst in the play, which is in response to the Nurse's advice to her to marry Paris as Romeo, after his banishment, is as good as dead:

> Ancient damnation! O most wicked fiend!
> Is it more sin to wish me thus forsworn,

Or to dispraise my lord with that same tongue
Which she had praised him with above compare.

So many thousand times? Go counselor!
Thou and my bosom henceforth shall be twain.
(III. v. 237–42)

Juliet feels outraged and expresses her anger and agony in this outburst but only after the exit of the Nurse. She calls the Nurse an old damnable woman, a wicked witch but all this is not within her earshot, which speaks volumes of her refinement. The difference between her refinement and the Nurse's crudity verging on obscenity is obvious in the latter's longish speech in which she describes the past, employs expressions like 'fall backward' (ready for sex), 'dug' (breast), nipple, and reproduces a sexual remark by her husband. (I.iii. 79–83)

Romeo is not as refined as Juliet but he is certainly more refined than his friend Mercutio whose language is nearly the most vulgar when he speculates on the physical relationship between his friend and Juliet. In reply to Benvolio's remark that Romeo's love for Juliet is blind, Mercutio says:

If love be blind, love cannot hit the mark
Now will he sit under a medlar tree
And wish his mistress were that kind of fruit
As maids call medlar when they laugh alone
O, Romeo, that she were, O that she were
An open arse and thou a popp'ring pear. (II. i. 33–38)

It is enough to say that the medlar, a small brown apple, is a slang for the vulva and poppering pear, a phallic-shaped pear is a slang for the erect penis. Now we can see how sharply Juliet contrasts with the Nurse and Romeo with Mercutio.

Mr and Mrs Capulet, Juliet's parents, called simply by the family name as Capulet and Capulet's wife, are also differentiated although their naming gives the impression that there is hardly any difference between the two. Mrs Capulet, like Juliet, is more in control of her emotion than her husband, though she is not quite as refined as her daughter. The one occasion where Mr. Capulet controls his emotion is at the party. Tybalt identifies Romeo and is going to kill him when Capulet firmly dissuades him from doing so. But this is not his tolerance but practical wisdom and self-interest, as he knows that any untoward incident will disrupt the party and deprive his daughter of the opportunity to interact with the young men and choose one of them, hopefully Paris, as her husband. However, in his relationship with his daughter, he is much harsher than his wife. Mrs Capulet tries and tries hard to persuade Juliet to marry Paris after Romeo is banished to Mantua but her husband threatens her in a language which does not behove a father:

> Hang thee, young baggage! disobedient wretch!
> I tell thee what—get thee to church a Thursday
> Or never after look me in the face.
>
> Speak not, reply not, do not answer me!
> My fingers itch. Wife, we scarce thought us blest
> That God lent us but this only child;
> But now I see this one is one too much
> And that we have a curse in having her. (III. v. 161–68)

His wife finds his language too hot and the Nurse blames him for berating Juliet in such strong language. But instead of cooling down, Mr. Capulet becomes harsher still:

> Graze thee where you will, you shall not house with me.
> Look to't; think on't; I do not use to jest
> Thursday is near, lay hand on heart, advise,
> An you be mine, I'll give you to my friend;

An you be not, hang, beg, starve, die in the streets
For, by my soul, I'll never acknowledge thee,
Nor what is mine shall never do thee good. (III.v. 190–96)

On her knees and with folded hands, Juliet begs her father to give her patient hearing but in response she gets only such strong reprimand. She keeps her cool but her father is all anger and fury passing judgement without listening.

We have seen how successfully Shakespeare has differentiated between the characters in the play placing Juliet at the centre as the most accomplished and refined of all.

The third element of drama, according to Aristotle, is thought which takes different forms in a play. Thought is expressed by the characters in communicating their ideas, arguments and counterarguments. It is at the centre of the universe created by the playwright coordinating its various emotions and ideas. The dialogue form makes a drama a series of speeches by the characters and each speech expresses ideas or refutation of ideas. It is the element of thought which differentiates one character from another, Romeo from Juliet and Capulet from his wife, for example. The thought-pattern in *Romeo and Juliet* is embodied in the movement of the action from enemity to reconciliation, which is also the overall pattern of the Shakespearean oeuvre from *Titus Andronicus* to *The Tempet*. The two families, the Capulets and the Mantagues, which have been at daggers drawn finally decide to forget their animosity, come to terms with each other, and live together happily.

Speaking of language, which is the last constituent of drama, one can say that Shakespeare excels all dramatists, ancient and modern, in the use of language. T.S. Eliot, himself a celebrated author of poetic drama, has significantly commented on the use of poetry in Shakespeare's drama:

> When Shakespeare introduced what might seem a purely poetic line or passage, it never interrupts the action, or is out of character, but on the contrary, in some mysterious way supports both action and character. (83)

Poetry in drama has to be dramatically justified which is best illustrated in the plays of Shakespeare. Shakespeare has assigned poetry according to the status of characters and it always reveals some trait of the character who employs it and advances the action of the play. The eponymous heroes of Shakespeare's tragedies always speak the best poetry. In *Romeo and Juliet,* the two eponymous characters, the hero and the heroine, speak the most poetic language which sheds significant light on their character and thought. Romeo swears by the moon to express his love for Juliet who rejects it because the moon is inconstant and asserts that there is no need for a contract at this stage of their love as it is

> Too rash, too unadvised, too sudden
> Too like the lightning, which both cease to be
> Ere one can say 'It lightens.' Sweet, good night!
> This bud of love, by summer's ripening breath,
> May prove a beauteous flower when next we meet. (II.ii. 118–22)

This is Juliet's speech at her second meeting with Romeo, the first being at the party organized by the Capulets where they fall in love at first sight. Here images are highly suggestive: their burgeoning love is like the momentary light generated by the sudden flash of lightning in the sky or it is like a bud which has yet to ripen into flower. The images of lightning and bud express the nature of Juliet's love for Romeo at this stage as well as reveal traits of her personality. She knows and she tells Romeo how deeply she is in love with him, but she is not swept off her feet by the upsurge of this feeling, as she knows that her love has yet to mature. Unlike Romeo, she is in control of her emotion. The imagery also presages the future course of action when their love will mature leading to their marriage. The language of the play is shot through with such powerful and highly suggestive images which reveal the feelings and the traits of the characters as well as advance the action of the play.

The reading of *Romeo and Juliet* in the light of Aristotle's concept of drama tells us much more about the play than Derrida's philosophical approach premised on aporia. Owing to his philosophical preoccupation, which sees no difference between literature and non-literature, he is incapable of responding to a complex and powerful work of literature like *Romeo and Juliet* which he reduces to a philosophical discourse on time and naming. Time and naming matter but they are not as important as the theme of love and death which is at the centre of the play uniting all the elements and constituents into an organic whole.

Note

1. All citations from *Romeo and Juliet* refer to the text edited by Peter Holland. New York: Penguin Books, 2000. Subsequent references have been incorporated in the text.

Works Cited

Bloom, Harold. *Shakespeare: The Invention of the Human.* New York: Riverhead Books, 1998.

Derrida, Jacques. *Acts of Literature,* ed. Derek Attridge. London: Routledge, 1991.

Eliot, T.S. *On Poetry and Poets.* London: Faber and Faber, 1971.

Bibliography

Abrams, M.H. 'Construing and Deconstructing'. In *Essays in Modern Criticism*, eds. Rajnath and William I. Elliott. Allahabad: Kitab Mahal, 1976; Delhi: Doaba House, 2006.

——. 'The Deconstructive Angel'. In *Contemporary Criticism,* ed. V.S. Saturaman. Madras: Macmillan India, 1979.

——. *A Glossary of Literary Terms.* Orlando: Harcourt Brace, 1999.

——. 'How to do Things with Texts?' *In Contemporary Criticism,* ed. V.S. Seturaman. Madras: Macmillan India, 1979.

——. *The Mirror and the Lamp.* London: Oxford University Press, 1979.

——. 'What is a Humanistic Criticism?' *Journal of Literary Criticism,* Vol. VII (December, 1996).

Anandavardhana. *DhvanyaLoka,* trans. and ed. K. Krishnamoorthy. Delhi: Motilal Banarasidass, 1982.

Austin, J.L. *How to Do Things with Words.* Cambridge, Mass.: Harvard University Press, 1975.

Bas, Alan. '"Literature"/Literature'. In *Velocities of Change,* ed. Richard Macksey, Baltimore: The Johns Hopkins University Press, 1974.

Bharat. *Natyasastra,* trans. Adya Rangacharya. New Delhi: Munshiram Manoharlal, 2007.

Bakhtin, M.M. *The Dialogic Imagination,* trans. Caryl Emerson, ed. Michael Holquist. Austin: University of Texas Press, 1983.

Bloom, Harold. *Shakespeare: The Invention of The Human.* New York: Riverhead Books, 1998.

Brooks, Cleanth. 'Irony as a Principle of Structure'. In *Literary Opinion in America,* ed. M.D. Zabel. New York: Harper Torchbooks, 1962.

——. 'The Primacy of the Linguistic Medium'. In *Contemporary Criticism,* ed. V.S. Seturaman. Madras: Macmillan India, 1979.

——. and R.P. Warren. *Understanding Poetry.* New York: Holt, Rinehart and Winston 1976.

——. *The Well-Wrought Urn.* New York: Brace and World, 1947.

Chari, V.K. *Sanskrit Criticism.* Delhi: Motilal Banarasidass, 1993.

Coleridge, S.T. *Biographia Literaria.* ed. J. Shawcross. London: Oxford University Press, 1967.

——. *Lectures and Notes on Shakespeare and other English Poets,* ed. T. Ash. London: G. Bells, 1908.

——. 'The Statesman's Manual.' In *The Political Tracts of Wordsworth, Coleridge, and Shelley,* ed. R.I. White. London: Cambridge University Press, 1953.

Culler, Jonathan. *Framing the Sign.* Oxford: Basil Blackwell, 1988.

——. *In Pursuit of Sings.* Ithaca: Cornell University Press, 1981.

——. 'Linguistics as a Model for Poetics.' In *Twentieth Century American Criticism: Interdisciplinary Approaches,* ed. Rajnath. New Delhi: Arnold-Heinemann, 1977.

——. *On Deconstruction.* London: Routledge and Kegan Paul, 1983.

——. *Structuralist Poetics.* Ithaca: Cornell University Press, 1975.

Dash, Irene G. *Wooing, Wedding and Power: Women in Shakespeare's Plays.* New York: Columbia University Press, 1981.

De Man, Paul. *Allegories of Reading*. New Haven: Yale University Press, 1979.

——. *Blindness and Insight.* New York: Oxford University Press, 1971.

Duvenage, Pieter. *Habermas and Aesthetics: The Limits of Communicative Reason*. Cambridge: Polity Press, 2003.

Derrida, Jacques. *The Act of Literature,* trans. and ed. Derek Attridge. London: Routledge, 1991.

——. *Dissemination,* trans. Barbara Johnson. London: Continuum, 1980.

——. 'Is there a Philosophical Language?' In *The Derrida, Habermas Reader,* ed. Lasse Thomassen. Edinburgh: Edinburgh University Press, 2006.

——. 'Living on: Borderlines'. In *Deconstruction and Criticism*, ed. Harold Bloom et al. New York: Continuum, 1979.

——. *Margins of Philosophy,* trans. Alan Bass. Sussex: Hanvester Press, 1982.

——. *Of Grammatology,* trans. Gayatri Chakraverty Spivak. Baltimore: The Johns Hopkins University Press, 1976.

——. 'White Mythology.' *New Literary History,* IV, Autumn, 1974.

——. *Writing and Difference,* trans. Alan Bass. London: Routledge, 2001.

Eco, Umberto. *On Literature,* trans. Martin McLaughlin. London: Vintage, 2006.

——. *A Theory of Semiotics.* Bloomington: Indiana University Press, 1976.

Eichenbaum, Boris. 'The Theory of the Formal Method.' In *Russian Formalist Criticism,* ed. L.T. Lemon and Marian J. Reiss. Lincoln: University of Nebraska Press, 1965.

Ellis, John. *Against Deconstruction.* Princeton: Princeton University Press, 1977.

Eliot, T.S. *On Poetry and Poets.* London: Faber and Faber, 1971.

——. *The Sacred Wood.* London: Methuen, 1967.

——. *Selected Essays.* London: Faber and Faber, 1951.

——. *T.S. Eliot: Selected Essays.* Introduction by Rajnath. Delhi: Doaba House, 2008.

Fish, Stanley. *Doing What Comes Naturally.* Cambridge, Mass.: Harvard University Press, 1989

——. *Is there a Text in this Class?* Cambridge, Mass.: Harvard University Press, 1980.

Fogle, R.H. *The Imagery of Keats and Shelley.* Hamden: Archan Books, 1962.

Frye, Northrop. *Anatomy of Criticism.* Princeton: Princeton University Press, 1971.

Frye, Paul H. *A Defence of Poetry.* California: Stanford University Press, 1955.

Gardner, Helen. 'Present Discontents.' In *Contemporary Criticism,* ed. V.S. Seturaman. Madras: Macmillan India, 1979.,

Gaynesford, Maximilian De. 'The Seriousness of Poetry.' *Essays in Criticism,* Vol. LIX, January, 2009.

Habermas, Jürgen. *The Philosophical Discourse of Modernity.* Cambridge: Polity Press, 1987.

——. 'Levelling the Genre Distinction between Philosophy and Literature.' In *The Derrida Habermas Reader,* ed. Lasse Thomassen. Edinburgh: Edinburgh University Press, 2006.

Heilman, R.B. *This Great Stage: Image and Structure in King Lear.* Seattle: University of Washington Press, 1962.

Hiriyanna. 'Some Aspects of India Aesthetics.' In *Indian Aesthetics,* ed. V.S. Saturaman. Madras: Macmillian India, 1964.

Holland, Norman N. *The Dynamics of Literary Response.* New York: Oxford University Press, 1968.

——. *The Critical I.* New York: Columbia University Press. 1992.

Hyman, S.E. *The Armed Vision.* New York: Vintage Books, 1955.

Jakobson, Roman. 'Linguistics and Poetics'. In *Style in Language,* ed. Thomas E. Sebeok. Cambridge, Mass.: MIT Press, 1960.

——. 'The Metaphoric and Metonymic Poles.' In *Modern Criticism and Theory,* ed. David Lodge. Delhi: Pearson 2004.

Kermode, Frank. *The Romantic Image.* London: Routledge and Kegal Paul, 1936.

Kernan, Alvin. *The Death of Literature.* New Haven: Yale University Press, 1990.

Krieger, Murray. 'Literature versus Ecriture: Constructions and Deconstructions in Recent Critical Theory'. In *Contemporary Criticism,* ed. V.S. Saturaman. Madras: Macmillan India, 1989.

Krishnamoorthy, K. *The Dhvanyaloka and its Critics.* Mysore: Kavyalaya Publishers, 1968.

K. Krishnamoorthy. Introduction, *Dhvanyaloka.* Delhi: Motilal Banarasidass, 1982.

Leavis, F.R. *Revaluation.* Harmondsworth: Penguin Books, 1964.

——. Compiled by. *A. Selection from Scrutiny,* Vols. 1 and 2. Cambridge: Cambridge University Press 1968.

Leitch, Vincent B. *Deconstructive Criticism: An Advanced Introduction.* New York: Columbia University Press, 1983.

Lemon, L.T. and Marion, J. Reiss. ed. *Russian Formalist Criticism.* Lincoln: University of Nebraska Press, 1965.

Lewis, C.D. *The Poetic Image. London:* Jonathan Cape, 1955.

Lotman, Jürij. *The Structure of the Artistic Text,* trans. Gail Lenhoff and Renold Vroon. Michgan: The University of Michigan Press, 1977.

Macksey, Richard. ed. *The Structuralist Controversy: The Languages of Criticism and the Sciences of Man.* Baltimore: The Johns Hopkins University Press, 1970.

——. *Velocities of Change.* Baltimore: The Johns Hopkins University Press, 1974.

McLeish, Archibald. *Poetry and Experience.* Harmondsworth: Penguin Books, 1965.

Malpas, Simon. *The Postmodern.* London: Routledge, 2007.

Marcuse, Herbert. *The Aesthetic Dimension.* Boston: Beacon Press, 1978.

Marsh, Florence. *Wordworth's Imagery.* New Haven: Yale University Press, 1952.

Matilal, Bimal Krishna. *The Word and the World.* New Delhi: Oxford University Press, 2001.

Mikics, David. *Who was Jacques Derrida*? New Haven: Yale University Press 2009.

Mohanty, S.P. *Literary Theory and the Claims of History.* New Delhi: Oxford University Press, 1998.

Norris, Christopher. *Deconstruction: Theory and Practice.* London: Methuen, 1982.

Plato. *Ion.* In *Ancient Literary Criticism,* ed. D.A. Russell and M. Wintenbottom. London: Oxford University Press, 1972.

——. *The Republic,* trans. Desmond Lee. Harmondsworth: Penguin Books, 1974.

Posner, Richard A. *Law and Literature.* Cambridge, Mass.: Harvard University Press, 2009. Chapter I, 'Literary Texts as Legal Texts'.

Rajnath. *Critical Speculations.* Delhi: Doaba House, 1996.

——. 'Creativity and Criticism.' *Indian Journal of English Studies,* Vol. LIV, 2017.

——. ed. *Deconstruction: A Critique.* London: Macmillan, 1989.

——. *Essays in Criticism.* Delhi: Doaba House, 1971; revised edition, 2004.

——. 'Introduction'. *T.S. Eliot: Selected Essays.* Delhi: Doaba Publications, 2008.

——. 'Literary Criticism in India'. *Journal of Literature and Aesthetics,* Vol. XVI, Jan. Dec. 2014.

——. *Nature Imagery of the Major Romantic Poets.* Varanasi: The Oriental Book Society, 1965; Delhi: Doaba House, 2014

Ransom. J.C. *Beating the Bushes.* New York: New Directions, 1972.

——. 'Criticism as Pure Speculation.' In *Essays in Modern Literary Criticism*, ed. R.B. West. New York: Rinehart, 1952.

——. *The World's Body.* Baton Rouge: Louisiana State University Press, 1968.

Kayan, Krishna. *Sahitya: A Theory.* New Delhi: Sterling, 1991.

——. *Suggestion and Statement in Poetry.* London: Athlone Press, 1972.

Richards, I.A. *Coleridge on Imagination.* London: Routedge, 1968.

——. *The Meaning of Meaning.* London: Routledge, 1952.

——. *The Philosophy of Rhetoric.* Oxford: Oxford University Press, 1936.

——. *Practical Criticism.* New York: Harcourt Brace Javanovich, 1929.

——. *Principles of Literary Criticism.* London: Routledge and Kegan Paul, 1955.

Richards, I.A. 'Science and Poetry.' In *Criticism,* ed. Mark Sehorer, M.G. Miles, G. Mckenzie. New York: Harcourt Brace, 1948.

Ricoeur, Paul. *The Rule of Metaphor,* trans. Robert Czerny. London: Routledge and Kegan Paul, 1978.

Roughley, Alan. *Reading Derrida Reading Joyce.* Gainesville: University Press of Florida, 1999.

Said, Edward. *The World, the Text and the Critic.* London: Vintage, 1991.

Sapir, Edward. *Culture, Language, and Personality,* ed. David G. Mandelbaum. Berkley: University of California Press, 1974.

Sartre, Jean Paul. *What is Literature?,* trans. Bernand Frechtman. London: Routledge, 1953.

Saussure, Ferdinand de. *Course in General Linguistics,* trans. Wade Baskin. New York: McGraw-Hill Book Company, 1966.

Scholes, Robert. *Structuralism in Literature.* New Haven: Yale University Press, 1974.

Searle, John. *Speech Acts: An Essay in the Philosophy of Language.* Cambridge. Cambridge University Press, 1969.

Seturaman, V.S. ed. *Contemporary Criticism.* Madras: Macmillan India, 1989.

Spivak, Gayatri Chakravorty. *A Critique of Postcolonial Reason.* Cambridge, Mass.: Harvard University Press; Calcutta: Seagull, 1999. Chapter 2. 'Literature' .

——. 'Translator's Preface,' *Of Grammatology.* Baltimore: The Johns Hopkins University Press, 1976.

Spurgeon, Caroline. *Shakespeare's Imagery.* Oxford: Clarendon Press, 1952.

Sreekantaiyya, T.N. *India Poetics,* trans. T. Balsubrahmanya. New Delhi: Sahitya Akademi, 2011.

Vološinov, V.N. *Marxism and the Philosophy of Language,* trans. Ladislav, Matejka and J.R. Titunik. New York: Seminar Press, 1973.

White, Hyden. *Metahistory: The Historical Imagination in Nineteenth-Century Europe.* Baltimore: The Johns Hopkins University Press, 1925.

——. *Tropics of Discourse.* Baltimore: The Johns Hopkins University Press, 1978.

White, James Boyd. *The Legal Imagination.* Abridged Edition. Chicago: University of Chicago Press, 1985. Chapter I. 'The Lawyer as Writer'.

Whorf, Benjamin Lee. *Language, Thought, and Reality,* Cambridge, Mass.: MIT Press, 1979.

Winters, Yvor. *In Defence of Reason.* Chicago: Swallow Press, 1937.

Wordsworth, William. 'Preface to *Lyrical Ballads.*' In *English Critical Texts,* ed. D.J. Enright and Ernst de Chickera. Delhi: Oxford University Press, 1978.

Index